Practical Parenting

A JEWISH PERSPECTIVE

Practical Parenting

A JEWISH PERSPECTIVE

by

Gail Josephson Lipsitz

KTAV Publishing House, Inc.

in association with

Jewish Family Services

1997

Library of Congress Cataloging-in-Publication Data

Lipsitz, Gail Josephson.
    Practical parenting : a Jewish perspective / by Gail Josephson Lipsitz.
        p.   cm.
    Includes bibliographical references.
    ISBN 0–88125–538–6
    1. Parenting—Religious aspects—Judaism. 2. Parenting—United
States. 3. Child rearing—United States. I. Title.
    HQ755.8.L55
        1977
    298.7'4—dc21   96-40372
                                                                              CIP

Manufactured in the United States of America
KTAV Publishing House, 900 Jefferson Street, Hoboken NJ, 07030

Contents

Acknowledgments

Practical Parenting: A Jewish Perspective grew out of a monthly feature series on parenting in the *Baltimore Jewish Times*. Undertaken through a special agreement between Jewish Family Services of Central Maryland, Inc., and the *Baltimore Jewish Times*, my column offered insights and practical advice on issues that parents typically face, presented within a Jewish context. Drawing on the clinical expertise of social workers from Jewish Family Services, and applying Jewish concepts and traditions to family relationships and contemporary life, I endeavored to make this material accessible and helpful to parents, professionals, and others involved in family life.

The original articles were amplified for this book, and bibliographies have been added. The vignettes, which are based on interviews with people in the community, use fictitious names and disguise some identifying information out of respect for privacy. The local educators, rabbis, and other professionals cited are identified by name with their consent. Unless otherwise stated, agencies, programs, synagogues and other institutions mentioned refer to the community of Baltimore, Maryland.

Many people were involved in the genesis of this volume. Each of the social workers from Jewish Family Services who collaborated with me provided vital parts of the book's foundation. Their knowledge and enthusiasm made me proud to be part of an agency with such an outstanding staff of professionals. I also gratefully acknowledge the encouragement and support of Dr. Lucy Y. Steinitz, Jewish Family Services' Executive Director from 1983 through 1996; Karen Nettler, Deputy Executive Director; and Susan Goldstein, Director of Child, Adolescent and Adult Services. My special thanks to Harriet Shiffman for her untiring assistance, word processing skills, and patience with the process of revision; and to Maureen Davidov and Marilyn Perlman, also of Jewish Family Services, for their help.

I thank the Baltimore rabbis, educators, and other Jewish professionals who contributed their knowledge and experience to this book. In particular, Rabbi Daniel Lehmann, formerly Upper School principal of the Beth Tfiloh Community School in Baltimore, and now founding headmaster of the New Jewish High School of Greater Boston, was an invaluable resource, giving many hours to reading selected chapters, providing connections to Jewish texts, and offering suggestions which strengthened and enriched the Jewish perspectives in the book. Ned Himmelrich gave generously of his time and guidance about the publishing process.

This book really came about because of the encouragement of my dear friend, Susan C. Goldberg of West Hartford, Connecticut. Her conviction that the original articles were of interest and value to a larger audience was the impetus. "A faithful friend is a secure shelter; whoever finds one has found a treasure" (Wisdom of Ben Sira). Many other friends kindly shared their personal experiences.

For embracing the original idea of a parenting series and sustaining it with encouragement over the three years represented in this book, my thanks to Gary Rosenblatt, former editor of the *Baltimore Jewish Times*, and Michael Davis, the current editor. For supporting the idea and collaborating on the publication of this book, I thank the Association of Jewish Family and Children's Agencies and its Executive Director, Bert Goldberg. It has been a special pleasure to work with KTAV Publishing House, Inc.

I humbly acknowledge the great wealth of wisdom about family life and parenting which exists in the writings of past and contemporary authors, and specifically the authors and publishers of particular works which have been cited. One wonderful resource into which I dipped many times to find quotations that crystallized Jewish thought on various subjects is *Voices of Wisdom: Jewish Ideals and Ethics for Everyday Living* by Francine Klagsbrun (Jonathan David Publishers, Inc., 1980). *Yiddish Proverbs*, edited by Hanan J. Ayalti (Schocken Books, 1963) also provided many gems.

Finally, deepest thanks to my parents, Elise and Neil Josephson, from whose love and skill at parenting I have always benefitted; to my husband, Allan Lipsitz, for his never-failing support, insights and editorial suggestions; and to our son, David Kiran, who has enabled us to share in the joys of parenting and family life, and whose ideas and voice animate much of this book.

"Each child carries his own blessing into the world," says a Yiddish proverb. Together with the staff of Jewish Family Services, I hope that this book will help those who parent, educate, and work with children, as they experience both the challenges and blessings that children bring with them.

Gail Josephson Lipsitz

Permissions

The author and publisher thank the following for permission to reprint:

Associated University Presses: Selection from Rufus Learsi, *Filled with Laughter: A Fiesta of Jewish Folk Humor*, 1961.

Bantam Doubleday Dell: Selections from Francine Klagsbrun, *Mixed Feelings: Love, Hate, Rivalry, and Reconciliation among Brothers and Sisters*, Bantam Books, 1993. Selections from Sharon Strassfeld and Kathy Green, *The Jewish Family Book*, Bantam Books, Copyright ©1981 by Sharon Strassfeld and Kathy Green.

Crown Publishers, Inc.: Selection from Lissy Jarvik, M.D., Ph.D. and Gary Small, M.D. *Parentcare: A Commonsense Guide for Adult Children*, Crown Publishers. Copyright ©1988 by Lissy Jarvik, M.D., Ph.D., and Gary Small, M.D.

The Free Press, a Division of Simon and Schuster: Selections from "Jewish Fathering" by Ari Goldman. In *The Hadassah Magazine Jewish Parenting Book*, edited by Roselyn Bell. Copyright ©1989 by Hadassah, The Women's Zionist Organization of America, Inc. Reprinted with permission of The Free Press, a Division of Simon and Schuster.

Sunie Levin: Selections from *Mingled Roots: A Guide for Jewish Grandparents of Interfaith Children*, Copyright ©1991 by Sunie Levin.

National Center for Learning Disabilities, Inc.: Poem by Emily Gross, Reprinted with the permission of the National Center for Learning Disabilities, 381 Park Avenue South, New York, NY 10016.

The Rabbinical Assembly: Selections reprinted from *Feast of Freedom*, pages 38 and 33, editor Rachel Anne Rabinowicz, 1982, Rabbinical Assembly. Reprinted with permission.

Schocken Books, Inc.: Selections from Rabbi Harold Kushner, *When Children Ask About God*, Copyright ©1989 by Harold S. Kushner.

Simon & Schuster: Selection reprinted with the permission of Simon & Schuster from *Meditations for Parents Who Do Too Much* by Wendy and Jonathon Lazear. Copyright ©1993 by Wendy Lazear and Jonathon Lazear. Selections reprinted with the permission of Simon & Schuster from *Money Doesn't Grow on Trees* by Neale S. Godfrey. Copyright ©1994 by Childrens Financial Network Incorporated.

Transaction Publishers: Selections from *Grandparents/Grandchildren: The Vital Connection* by Arthur Kornhaber, M.D. and Kenneth L. Woodward, Copyright ©1991 by Arthur Kornhaber and Kenneth L. Woodward.

United Synagogue of America, Department of Youth Activities: Selection from Rabbi Carl Astor, . . . *Who Makes People Different: Jewish Perspectives on the Disabled*, 1985. Selections from Rabbi Jack Moline, *Jewish Leadership and Heroism*, 1987.

Viking Penguin: Selection from *First Feelings* by Stanley and Nancy T. Greenspan. Copyright ©1985 by Stanley Greenspan, M.D., and Nancy Thorndike Greenspan. Used by permission of Viking Penguin, a division of Penguin Books USA, Inc.

W. W. Norton & Company, Inc.: Selection from Erik Erikson, *Childhood and Society*, 1963.

Many Kinds of Families

The One and Only

At the market, Stacey unexpectedly meets Janice, an old friend who just recently moved back to town. Stacey introduces Janice to Miriam, her six-year-old daughter. "She's darling," bubbles Janice. "Is she your only one?"

"Why is it," Stacey later wonders to her husband, "that responses like that always make me feel apologetic about having *only* one child—as if one isn't good enough?"

Indeed, society's reactions indicate a strong expectation that parents will produce at least two children. This attitude is prevalent in American culture, but especially in Jewish tradition. "*P'ru u'rvu*"—Be fruitful and multiply"—is the first Biblical commandment (Genesis 1:28). Children are seen as the greatest blessing, a sign of God's favor (Leviticus 26:9). *Halachah* (Jewish law) requires couples to strive for at least one female and one male offspring (Maimonides, *Hilchot Ishut*, ch. 15).

Contemporary Jewish leaders express a wide range of views on this subject. Rabbi Ervin Preis of Suburban Orthodox Congregation, for example, believes that modern Jews have an historic obligation to promote Jewish continuity, in part to replenish our people after the devastating losses of the Holocaust. "Jewish survival is incumbent upon all of us," says Rabbi Floyd Herman of Har Sinai Congregation, "and how many children we have is a part of this. That is a deeply personal decision."

In spite of Judaism's emphasis on procreation, the birth rate among American Jews today has dropped below the population replacement level. According to the National Jewish Population Survey published by the Council of Jewish Federations in 1990, 30.3% of all adult Jewish women over age 18 had no children, and 16.2% had one child. Less than 24% had three or more children. In addition, of the 2.7% of women ages 18–44 who were adoptive parents, 60% had adopted one child.

People have only one child for a variety of reasons. The growing divorce rate has curtailed child bearing in some families. In marriages that are intact, financial pressures can influence many couples to stop at one child. Both parents may have to work full-time to meet expenses. Others may wish to avoid a prolonged interruption in their careers for child-rearing. Elaine, the mother of a high school student, reflects, "We've been able to juggle professional and family life, maintaining our chosen lifestyle and giving our son many opportunities without being stretched to the limit." The standard of living many parents choose today includes increasingly high costs for Jewish education, synagogue membership, private school, summer camp, and college education—costs they feel are affordable for only one child.

Some parents decide to have one child for philosophical reasons. Elliot and Nancy wanted to experience parenthood, but worry about the overpopulation of the world. "We feel completely fulfilled as parents of one," says Elliot. Others limit their child-bearing because of medical factors, such as risks of pregnancy for the woman or known genetic risks to an unborn child.

Many couples, however, would have liked more children, but have had one, by birth or adoption, only after a long struggle with infertility. With more Jewish adults postponing marriage and child-bearing, fertility problems now affect about one Jewish couple in five. For women like Stacey, who gave birth to Miriam when she was 38 and who has had several miscarriages, questions like "Do you have any others?" stir up painful feelings. Still, Stacey and Alex feel lucky to be parents at all. Parents for whom infertility remains a troubling issue can benefit from professional counseling. They may also wish to consider alternative ways, such as adoption, to build a family.

A long period of barrenness, followed by the birth of a very much wanted child to whom high expectations are attached, is a recurrent theme in the Bible, and one that resonates with meaning for parents today. On Rosh Hashanah, we read of two such families: Abraham and Sarah, who gave birth to Isaac, and Hannah and Elkanah, who bore Samuel and dedicated him to God's service.

Divine intervention enabled Sarah, at the age of 90, finally to conceive a child with Abraham (then age 100). No wonder Abraham and Sarah named their only son Isaac, which, in Sarah's words, means "God has brought me laughter." God promised that, through Isaac, Abraham and Sarah would "become a great and populous nation."

Then, several years later, in the ultimate test of the patriarch's faith, God tells Abraham: "Take your son, *your only son* whom you love, even Isaac . . . and offer him for a burnt offering . . ." (Why the focus is on Abraham's only son with Sarah, thus ignoring his son Ishmael, born to his wife Hagar, is the subject of much rabbinic discussion.) This powerful, troubling story evokes any parent's worst nightmare. Losing one's child means losing a beloved being, the joys of parenthood, and one's link to the future. Although the human sacrifice is averted by God in response to Abraham's demonstration of faith, all of the protagonists are indelibly affected by the experience. Indeed, a legend tells us that the shock of learning that her son had narrowly escaped death, in fact, kills Sarah. (A strange counterpoint to this story appears in the book of Judges where Jephthah actually sacrifices his daughter—his only child—because of a rash vow he made to God.)

The Hebrew word "*yechid*," meaning "the only one," in God's command to Abraham about sacrificing Isaac, carries a range of connotations which are significant for parents today. "*Yechid*" can mean beloved or best-loved; a priceless and irreplaceable possession; favored, preferred above others, chosen, or unique. In some contexts, it also means solitary or lonely.

The child who is *yechid* experiences both special privileges and special challenges. Engaged in an intense relationship with his or her parents, this child frequently assumes the responsibility of meeting their high expectations. Indeed, single children tend to be high achievers. Survey examples from the cover personalities of *Time*

Magazine and *Who's Who* reveal that only children are over-represented as leaders in all categories. Environmental advantages can partly explain the rich potential and performance of only children, but they may also rise to others' expectations because there is no one else to do so.

Some of the popular conceptions of only children are less positive. They are often portrayed as lonely, egotistical, and spoiled. However, a 1980 study by Denise Polit, Ronald Nuttal, and Ena Nuttall found that single children were generally well-adjusted and had the same levels of perceived happiness and satisfaction as children with siblings.[1]

Only children are aware of the advantages and drawbacks of their situation. Seven-year-old Josh says, "If I had a brother or a sister, I wouldn't have to be so lonely playing. I think my parents would have enough love for two of us. But, most brothers and sisters do fight and make a lot of noise." Only children do not experience the close companionship and lifelong bonds of sibling relationships, and the opportunities to learn, in the family arena, skills of negotiation, conflict resolution, and responsibility for others. However, there is no evidence that this affects their ability to establish and maintain meaningful relationships.

Danny, age 17, has always been glad there was not another child in the house. "I haven't had to worry about favoritism or money. But my personality is a private one. I have the freedom to be who I am naturally and to invite friends over when I feel like it," he adds. Benefits mentioned by other "onlies" include having their own rooms, going on special excursions with their parents, and enjoying their parents' undivided attention when they want to talk about things that matter.

Elaine, a social worker who is Danny's mother, observes that, contrary to the stereotype, single children are generous and willing to share because they are not mandated to do this on a day-to-day basis. They have a fundamental sense of security because their needs

---

[1]Denise F. Polit, Ronald L. Nuttal, and Ena V. Nutall, "The Only Child Grows Up: A Look at Some Characteristics of Adult Only Children," *Family Relations,* January 1980.

are being met. Many only children also learn early to develop their own inner resources of imagination and initiative to entertain themselves. Elaine thinks that the loneliness of the only child is a myth. "The parents are more likely to be lonely when the child cultivates her own interests and friends away from home," she says. "But this can be an opportunity for spouses to pursue their own interests and to deepen their own bonds."

Children can grow and flourish in many kinds of families. Whether the family with one child was formed by choice or not, the important thing is that it be a loving family. "Next time someone asks me if Miriam is my only child," says Stacey, "I will say, Yes, and she is *one*-derful!"

Suggestions for Parents of One Child

1. Give your child opportunities to build relationships with other children. Invite friends in to play and stay overnight. Encourage participation in clubs and sports activities of his or her choice, scouts, synagogue youth groups, and summer programs.

2. Build an extended family of cousins and good friends.

3. Give your child times away from you to cultivate independence, such as overnight stays at the home of friends, playing with families who have several children, and sleepover camp.

4. Avoid placing unrealistic hopes, expectations, and pressure on your child. Too heavy a burden can result in a modern form of child sacrifice.

5. Plan for the future. Develop outside sources of support so that your child will not have to assume sole responsibility for the care of elderly parents.

Sibling Struggles

It's as old as Cain and Abel, Isaac and Ishmael, Jacob and Esau. It did not spare Rachel and Leah or Aaron, Miriam, and Moses. Joseph and his brothers had a bad case. And it's as new as the fight your children had at breakfast this morning over who got more syrup on his waffles.

Sibling rivalry can drive even the calmest parents to distraction. "They can't ever sit next to each other without fighting. It's totally exhausting," says Denise, mother of three boys ages 10 to 13. "They can be getting along just fine when they'll suddenly start to fight over nothing," adds Howard, whose son and daughter are 6 and 9. Some parents react with frustration and anger; others confess there are times they wish they'd stopped at one child.

Friction among siblings is indeed a common and urgent concern of parents. About 80% of people in the United States and Europe grow up with siblings. These ties endure longer than any other attachment we have, says Francine Klagsbrun, author of *Mixed Feelings: Love, Hate, Rivalry, and Reconciliation Among Brothers and Sisters*. Klagsbrun asserts that the sibling experience leaves an "indelible imprint on all areas of life," affecting our adult relationships from family and marriage to work and friendships.

Sibling rivalry is competition between children in the same family for the attention and affection of the significant people in their lives. Siblings may compete for the attention of any adult caring for them, but especially that of their parents. It begins when the firstborn child feels displaced after the second one arrives because he perceives, correctly, that he must now share a finite amount of parental energy and attention.

Some rivalries, however, can also occur independent of the parents. Children commonly argue over toys, likes and dislikes, which TV show to watch, and violations of their space. Denise's boys compare who's better at report cards, sports, anything at all. This struggle for power in relation to each other is an intrinsic part of sibling dynamics. Jacob and Esau were competitors in their mother's womb long before they even knew their parents. The Biblical paradigms are about reality, and these relationships show that sibling rivalry is deeply embedded in the human condition, says Rabbi Joel Mishkin of Temple Beth Shalom in Sarasota, Florida.

Relations among siblings are affected by many variables, including the nature of the parental relationship, the number of children in a family, their place in the family as determined by birth order, the number of years between them, and their sexes. Dr. Naomi Baumgarten, an educational and clinical psychologist, says that sibling rivalry is not necessarily diffused when there are more children. The potential for competition is likely to be greater with only two children. However, she points out that each child has a unique temperament and interacts in a different way in the family.

Although the term "sibling rivalry" conjures up negative associations for most parents, sibling relationships actually have many positive aspects. During childhood, says Francine Klagsbrun, brothers and sisters develop a "horizontal" relationship as peers that encourages freedom, openness, and intimacy. Siblings amass detailed knowledge of each other and a shared personal history that remain with them for life. In addition to confirming for each other certain realities about their parents, thereby freeing each other of unnecessary guilt, Klagsbrun notes that siblings become allies who "offer each other solace and safety in a world stacked in favor of adults."

Sibling rivalry is a normal and necessary socialization process, the beginning of children's achieving a sense of independence from their parents and acquiring skills useful in future relationships with peers and in adult life. Says Dr. Baumgarten, "Sibling relations can strengthen a child's ability to enter into the competitive arena, if the parents provide the necessary degree of T.L.C. so that the child doesn't have to compete for a sense of well being."

Additional positive products of sibling rivalry are negotiation and mediation skills and a sense of responsibility for others, which can be transferred from the family to later relationships and positions such as team captain and organization president. Finally, siblings learn to develop the empathic responses of caring and understanding another's feelings which are essential to healthy relationships.

All of this takes the long view. Meanwhile, what is a parent to do while the kids are slugging it out in the back seat of the car?

Here are some helpful strategies. Professionals and parents alike agree on the importance of treating each child as an individual. Dr. Lee Salk, author of *What Every Child Would Like His Parents to Know*, counsels avoiding comparing your children, telling them instead that since everyone is different, no one ever loves two people in the same way.

Some Rabbinic commentators point out that Jacob may have been responsible for the sibling tension between Joseph and his brothers as a result of the preferential treatment he gave to his favorite son, Joseph. Children need to feel that they are loved equally, even while their needs for parental attention may be very different.

"Fair" treatment is not the same as "equal" treatment. "Fair" means serving each child's unique needs. An older brother can stay out later; a younger child may need a bedtime story while the older one does his homework. A child with a learning disability needs more parental help on some tasks that her sister can do for herself. On the other hand, be sure that each child's roles are balanced so his own needs are met. If the eldest has more responsibility at home, arrange to attend his big soccer game by getting a sitter for the baby.

To offset what children perceive as inequality or injustice, try to give significant individual time to each child. An outing shared with one parent, when the child has that parent's full attention, goes a long way toward enhancing a developing self-image. Try to make time for each child alone with a parent before bed, to read, to talk, or just to cuddle.

Invite, and then listen non-defensively to what is on your child's mind. You show respect for your child if you allow her to say, "Can't we send the baby back?" without laughing or scolding her that she "shouldn't feel that way." Encouraging the expression of feelings, showing you understand while gently explaining the realities, helps prevent the explosion of feelings into hostile acts later.

Think and act preventively. Understanding your child's developmental level helps avoid setting up situations beyond his ability to control. Prepare a toddler for the arrival of a new sibling, and schedule a regular special activity with the older one after the baby arrives. Try not to put any child in a situation in which he cannot control his frustration, such as leaving a three-year-old alone with the new baby.

Allow siblings to work out their own differences as much as possible. Dr. Baumgarten observes that in the normal give and take of sibling interaction, parental siding is not necessarily the most effective approach. It is more important to recognize each child's feelings. If the conflict spills over into physical violence, however, separate the fighters, and impose a time-out period for cooling off, each one in a separate area. Make clear what behavior is unacceptable. Exclusion from the social unit of the family is more effective than punishment.

Don't feel you have failed as a parent when your children fight with each other and compete for your attention. However, if the behavior is out of control, interfering with your child's productive functioning and with his sense of self-esteem, or if your child seems totally unable to share the attention of an adult or to share belongings, it is time to seek help from your pediatrician or a child guidance professional.

Childhood sibling rivalries may never be "resolved" completely. Indeed, the ancient Biblical tales illustrate the complexity of the sibling relationship. In a famous *midrash*, one rabbi questioned the apparent simplicity of Jacob and Esau's reconciliation as adults, suggesting that when Esau fell upon Jacob's neck, his embrace was more a bite than a kiss!

And yet, the book of Genesis concludes only after a significant reconciliation is achieved between Joseph and his brothers, points out Rabbi Daniel Lehmann: "While Judaism recognizes the inherent tension that often exists between siblings, it understands that healthy families, and ultimately a healthy people, can only be built upon a foundation of sibling love."

The best that parents can do is to build the groundwork for life-long healthy relationships among their children by respecting the individuality and uniqueness of each and by teaching them to acknowledge and control their rivalries.

Smoothing the Path for Siblings

1. Remember that each child is unique and deserves your special attention to his or her feelings and needs. Emphasize that you will treat your children fairly, not necessarily equally.

2. Avoid getting in the middle of sibling rivalries. Encourage your children to develop their own conflict resolution skills.

3. Foster respect in each child for siblings, helping each to see the special needs and strengths of the other.

4. Read books that highlight sibling issues with your children to show them they are not alone in dealing with these problems and to give them opportunities to express their feelings.

5. Recall your own earlier experiences as a sibling, how your parents handled the struggles, and how you felt in situations similar to those in which your children are engaged.

6. Encourage a sense of the family as a unit on occasions such as Shabbat and holidays, and by planning outings and activities together. In spite of their fighting, siblings will have good memories of these family times.

Adoption: Another Way to Grow a Family

A conversation overheard by Joanne between her daughter, Jennifer, and a visiting playmate, Beth, both age 7:

> JENNIFER: "Beth, why don't you look like your Mom and Dad?"
> BETH: "Because I am Korean. My American Mom and Dad adopted me."
> JENNIFER: "What's adopted?"
> BETH: "It means I needed a family and my parents needed a child. So now I'm part of their family forever."

After Beth leaves, Jennifer says, "Mom, Beth told me she was adopted. Why did her real parents in Korea give her away? Didn't they love her?" Later, Joanne tells her husband, "I didn't know how best to answer Beth's questions. I guess I don't fully understand adoption myself."

Most families these days know someone who has adopted a child. Since the 1970s, adoption has become much more visible, largely because of the growth in international placements. More than 8,000 children were adopted from abroad in the United States in 1994. 2.7% of American Jewish families with children have adopted children, either domestically or internationally, according to the 1990 National Jewish Population Survey by the Council of Jewish Federations. With infertility now affecting one Jewish couple in five, the numbers of adoptive families are growing. Gone are the days when this subject was discussed in whispers. Adoptive parents today openly talk about adoption with their children, understanding that this is a vital part of their identity.

Being able to answer your child's questions about adoption in a helpful, accurate way means informing yourself first. It may also involve re-examining some assumptions. Families formed through adoption differ in some ways from other kinds of families, and many people equate "different" with "abnormal." Adoption is commonly perceived as a "second-best" way of making a family. Our culture tends to demean adoption through television dramas and sensationalized publicity about adopted children "gone bad," when in fact such cases are extremely rare. Well-meaning programs like "Adopt a highway" or "Adopt a zoo animal" trivialize the commitment to another human being that adoption requires.

"Adoption is simply another way to form a family—not better than or less than other ways," says Lois Ruskai Melina, an adoptive parent and author. In *Making Sense of Adoption*, Melina presents adoption as "a way of joining a family rather than as a description of a person." Adoptive families are normal, functional families, who form attachments as deep as those in biological families, according to the research of Dr. David Brodzinsky, a psychologist at Rutgers University.

This finding reinforces what Judaism has long known. The modern Hebrew word for adoption, *ametz*, meaning "strengthen," comes from a reference in Psalm 80 to a stem transplanted and made strong. The Biblical figures Eliezer, Moses, and Esther were all adopted. "Whoever raises an orphan in his home is credited by Scripture as if he had borne him," says the Talmud (*Megillah* 13a). In his book, *And Hannah Wept: Infertility, Adoption, and the Jewish Couple*, Rabbi Michael Gold quotes additional traditional sources showing that Judaism values the parent who nurtures and educates a child, regardless of whether that parent gave birth to the child.

Parents who adopt are motivated by diverse reasons. They include single adults who wish to have a family, people ideologically committed to population control, and couples who have struggled with infertility. The pain of Jewish couples who cannot bear children is intensified by constant reminders of how valued children are in the

Jewish tradition, as epitomized by the first Biblical commandment: "Be fruitful and multiply." As Lois Melina points out, infertile adopters prefer adopting rather than continuing with medical treatments or remaining childless. Most adoptive parents, she says, "don't consider adoption a *second-best* alternative, but a *second choice* that has turned out to be as acceptable as their first." Many Jewish adoptive parents find special meaning in Psalm 113, recited in the Hallel prayer: "He makes the childless woman to dwell in her house as a joyful mother of children."

How should parents explain adoption to their children? Brodzinsky's research found that children's ability to understand various aspects of adoption changes with their development. Our goal as parents is to provide information appropriate to our children's ability to absorb it in a meaningful way, according to their interest and emotional maturity.

If you know a couple who have adopted because of infertility, and your child has questions, here is a simple explanation: "Rachel and Bob wanted a baby very much, but they couldn't make one themselves. Beth was made by another man and woman. She grew inside that other woman and was born to her. Those people are called her birthparents."

When a child asks why the birthparents "gave up" their baby, an understandable answer is: "Beth's birthparents couldn't take care of *any* child born to them at that time in their lives. They were probably very sad about that, and they will never forget about Beth, but they thought that other parents could take better care of Beth at that time. When Rachel and Bob adopted Beth, she became part of their family forever."

This explanation makes several important points. First, it was the birthparents' problem that necessitated the adoption, rather than something wrong with the child. In addition, adoption satisfies needs of both the adoptive parents and the child, and is a permanent decision. Children should not be told that birthparents place their children for adoption out of love; they may conclude that parents who love children "give them away."

Language conveys attitudes. Suggested positive terms when discussing adoption include: "birthparents" (instead of "real" or "natural" parents); "place a child for adoption" or "make an adoption plan" (instead of "put up for adoption" or "give away"); and "choose to parent" (rather than "keep the baby"). Adopted children should not be presented as objects of pity, nor described romantically as "special" or "chosen."

Derogatory comments about minorities are especially hurtful to families who have adopted a child of a different race or ethnic group. Children in our community can be reminded that the Jewish family is an international one, comprised of people with a broad spectrum of ethnic backgrounds and physical appearances, as is readily apparent in Israel. Indeed, cross-cultural adoption is changing the face as well as perceptions of the American Jewish community as well.

When discussing adoption with older children, Myra Hettleman, LCSW-C, director of Jewish Family Services' Adoption Alliances, recommends acknowledging that adoption involves pain, as well as the joy of forming a family. Birthparents, adoptive parents, and adopted children (from about age 7) are all aware that they have experienced losses.

In addition, outsiders need to respect the adoptive family's right to privacy, particularly about details of the child's genetic and social history. Some information belongs to the adopted child, and the parents help him or her decide when and with whom to share it. Young children with normal curiosity should not be made to feel that adoption is a taboo or secret subject, but can be taught sensitivity to others.

If you overhear your child asking an adopted child questions, don't rush to intervene for fear the topic is too sensitive. Let the child answer for himself. Adoptive parents today receive guidance in how to explain adoption to their children, and most adopted youngsters will handle questions in a matter-of-fact way, or will deflect a question that makes them uncomfortable. Most adoptive parents would also welcome being given the opportunity to answer questions from other parents like, "How do you suggest I present adoption to my child?" and "What would you like me to tell Jennifer about Beth's adoption?"

Adoption is a complicated topic that is best dealt with in several conversations at different stages in your child's growth. Try to respond when your child brings up the subject or asks questions without making your answer a serious "lesson." You can also introduce the subject naturally into a conversation about different kinds of families, or read one of the numerous books for children available today on this subject. At ages 9 or 10, children who were not adopted often wonder or fantasize about having been adopted themselves. This is a good opportunity for parents to discuss different ways of building families without making value judgments.

Adoptive families are different, but like all kinds of families, they are built with lasting bonds of commitment and love. The more our children can understand and appreciate that each of us is unique, the better they will feel about themselves and about the ways in which they are different.

Helping Children Understand Adoption

1. Ask your child's school to find natural ways to incorporate education about adoption into the curriculum, such as during units on various kinds of families, multicultural programs, and social studies and science units on family history and genetics. Invite a parent from the local chapter of Stars of David International to come and speak. Stars of David International is the information and support network for Jewish and partly Jewish adoptive families. (Please see Resource list.)

2. Seek out books to read with your children that present families and adoption in terms appropriate for their developmental levels. Many bookstores and libraries have sections on the family and/or adoption.

3. Cultivate an awareness of the power of language and stereotypes to mold children's attitudes. Remember that our worldwide Jewish community is a diverse one, and make a special effort to welcome adopted children.

4. If you are at a loss about how to answer your child's questions about adoption, consulting a professional with expertise on the subject or an adoptive parent can be helpful.

The Family with a Difference: Children with Disabilities

"I am like a crystal prism,
With many different sides to me,
I can only achieve my rainbow,
When someone helps to provide me the light.
I sometimes feel as though I have been put in a dark room,
Where light is a privilege that must be earned instead of a right.
And where my rainbow is not always welcome.
Then sometimes, I feel the world is a blank page,
And I am there to spread my colors across it."[1]

These lines of poetry, written by a thirteen-year-old child with learning disabilities, express the feelings of isolation, frustration, and sadness that many children with special needs experience because they are often judged and labelled, instead of being appreciated for who they are and what they can do.

For these children and their families, the teaching in *Pirke Avot* (*Ethics of the Fathers* 4:27) has special meaning: "Do not judge by the container, but by what is inside."

Disabilities—whether severe or mild, physical or cognitive, psychological or behavioral, or combinations of these—present challenges for children, their families, and their community. Ideally, the common goal of families and all who interact with them is to help

---

[1]"Me," by Emily Gross, reprinted with permission of the National Center for Learning Disabilities, 381 Park Ave. South, NY, NY 10016

each child reach his or her potential and live a life of dignity, independence, and participation in the community to the fullest extent possible.

A child with special needs usually requires additional attention, energy and time from parents. Many hours may be spent in testing, evaluation, therapy, tutoring, and simply travelling to appointments. The Education for All Handicapped Children Act of 1975 (Public Law 94–142) mandates that the public school system provide a free and appropriate education for children with disabilities until age 22. However, negotiating the complex educational system to balance children's need for services with their need for inclusion can be overwhelming, says Rachel Howard, LCSW, director of Residential and Support Services for Jewish Family Services. While certain services should be provided through the school, the financial impact on the family can be significant. Parents often forego professional or educational opportunities for themselves or other family members because they must be available to advocate and care for a child with a disability. They also invest much time in keeping abreast of new developments related to their child's specific needs.

In addition, many of these families experience emotional stresses. Parents may grieve over the loss of the "normal" child about whom they dreamed. This pain can resurface at times that ordinarily would be developmental milestones. Beginning school and later, entering adolescence can be particularly challenging times. When children themselves perceive that their capabilities are limited, for example, when they have difficulty interacting with their peers, parents feel their pain, as well.

Contributing to family strains are differences in the way each parent reacts to the child's disability. Some can express their emotions, deal with the grief, accept the situation, and focus on the present. Others have difficulty acknowledging the existence or extent of a problem, or are unable to share their feelings of loss, anger, and guilt. Because parents have different ways of handling stress, they may not be able to offer support to each other. As a result, communication can deteriorate, affecting the marital relationship and, in turn, the entire family. Couples experiencing this degree of stress can benefit from marital therapy.

Adult extended family members also play an important role. When present, they can offer emotional support and assistance with caregiving. However, some relatives find it difficult to accept the reality that a child has disabilities, a reaction which can be especially painful to parents. Everyone most benefits when the whole family works together on behalf of the child. Parents can help themselves by putting their child's and their family's needs first, and planning appropriately. It may be necessary to educate extended family and friends to be more sensitive.

Families cope best when they begin addressing their situation early, says Audrey Leviton, LCSW, program manager for the Child and Family Support Program of the Kennedy Krieger Institute. In addition to home-based training, counseling, and other services, the program offers support groups that diminish the isolation felt by parents and other relatives of children with developmental disabilities, help them deal with feelings and learn coping strategies. "Families are the real experts on their child," says Leviton; at their request, professionals can provide support.

Jewish parents of children with special needs confront some unique issues, according to Marjorie Shulbank, coordinator of Child Find for the Maryland State Department of Education, Division of Special Education. To alleviate the isolation and stress families experience in trying to meet the complex needs of children with disabilities, Shulbank and occupational therapist Shani Goodman began the Maryland Association for Jewish Parents of Children with Disabilities, a support network for Shomer Shabbos families.

Families can connect their children with special needs to the Jewish community, first, by including them in their Jewish home life, points out Marci B. Dickman, Executive Director of the Council on Jewish Education Services (CJES). Participating in Shabbat and holiday preparations and rituals, and marking significant life cycle events with symbols their children can understand, are some ways to do this.

Judaism offers many opportunities for hands-on involvement that are very accessible to children with special needs—experiences such as making challah, eating matza, participating in Havdalah, and planting trees on Tu B'shvat, says Amian Frost Kelemer, Coordinator of the Department of Special Education at CJES.

"Judaism teaches that all Jews were at Sinai and received the Torah, and therefore all have a right to learn Torah," says Kelemer. The Jewish community, particularly synagogues and schools, can support families of children with special needs by welcoming and including them. We can also create programs and support existing ones that educate Jewish children in ways that are appropriate to their needs. Community schools such as P'TACH (Parents for Torah for All Children), which operate independently in several cities, and Gesher LaTorah of CJES enable students with unique learning needs, who cannot receive a formal Jewish education in regular classroom settings, to learn about Judaism and gain Jewish pride.

A wonderful benefit of a program like Gesher LaTorah, according to its principal, Amian Frost Kelemer, is that it affords children a chance to contribute to the community as Jews. For example, they can lead prayers in services, participate in a community mitzvah day, do *tikkun olam* by cleaning up the environment, or perform the *mitzvah* of *bikkur cholim* (visiting the sick). These are opportunities for children to be successful and proud of their accomplishments in their Jewish life. The common goal of these kinds of programs is the fullest possible participation of children with disabilities in Jewish home and community life.

One of the most significant milestones for a Jewish child with a disability is Bar or Bat Mitzvah. Melissa Silverman's story, featured as a cover article in the *Baltimore Jewish Times*,[1] is a beautiful and inspiring one.

Melissa, who has Down syndrome, became a Bat Mitzvah at Beth Am Congregation in November 1995. After leading the Torah service and reading from the Torah, Melissa spoke of how she'd wanted to become a Bat Mitzvah like other kids, at age 13. "My Bat Mitzvah is an example of how I want people to see me—as Melissa, someone who can do almost everything that other kids do. I do them slower and I have to work real hard to learn, but I can do almost everything . . . My Bat Mitzvah has been a challenge for me . . . a test of my faith in me."

---

[1]Michael Davis and Rebecca Shavulsky, "A Test of My Faith in Me," *Baltimore Jewish Times,* November 24, 1995, pp. 42-49.

Jay Silverman, Melissa's father, says, "We knew we wanted our child to be someone of high self-respect and respect for others . . . the kind of person who would always do her best at whatever she attempted. Those goals did not change when we learned she had Down Syndrome; they were only re-focused." "We never say to her, 'You can't do something,'" adds Melissa's mother Janis.

Melissa's determination and dedication enabled her to realize her dream. In this process, the involvement of her family, congregation and community can serve as a model. Melissa's teachers at Chizuk Amuno Preschool helped lay the foundation. Gesher LaTorah of CJES prepared her for undertaking, and provided additional support through, the more challenging studies for Bat Mitzvah. Her teacher for her big day was Cantor Beth Weiner, with support from Melissa's cousin Bonnie Stainman and from Cantor Susan Berkson.

At the service, after Rabbi Ira Schiffer spoke to Melissa, Cantor Weiner said, "Many people have guided and nurtured you to this day. There is an expression that it takes a community to raise a child. Today we see the truth of that saying. . . ."

One other important issue for parents to consider is how other children in a family are affected by having a sibling with disabilities. A range of reactions and concerns is typical. Children may have a hard time answering questions about why their sibling is different or dealing with teasing from peers. It is important for parents to allow their children to express their feelings and enable them to handle others' reactions. Brothers and sisters can also be encouraged to allow a sibling with disabilities to do for herself as much as she is able. While helping their other children relate to their sibling in positive ways, parents need to let them know that they are not expected to take on adult responsibilities. Brothers and sisters need respect for their privacy, opportunities to socialize with friends, and quality time alone with parents. They also benefit from sharing experiences and feelings with peers in special support groups like those offered by the Child and Family Support Program at Kennedy Krieger Institute. Audrey Leviton points out that these groups can identify and bolster the strengths of children who have siblings with disabilities, including greater sensitivity and understanding for others.

Contemporary families can learn much from the relationship of

Biblical siblings Moses and Aaron (Exodus 4–6). Moses' response
to the divine command to lead the Israelites out of slavery is that no
one will listen: "I am not a man of words . . . for I am slow of speech
and of a slow tongue." Whether Moses had a physical speech imped-
iment is unclear; we have a variety of rabbinic commentaries on this
passage. But Moses' *perception* of himself as one who does not speak
well certainly affects his self-confidence. God finally appoints Aaron
to be Moses' spokesman. The two siblings develop a dynamic part-
nership, leading their people to freedom. After the miraculous cross-
ing of the Red Sea, Moses composes a magnificent poem of praise
which he sings with the Israelites. With God's guidance and inspira-
tion, and through collaboration with his brother Aaron, Moses
builds on his strengths and discovers he can express his true potential as a leader.

The difficulties faced by families of children with disabilities "differ only in degree from those of other families," says Helen Featherstone in *A Difference in the Family: Living with a Disabled Child.* "One
child's disability reshapes every life in unexpected ways. Nonetheless . . . each makes a life—often a good one—out of a difference in
the family."

Suggestions for Parents of Children with Disabilities

1. Seek the support of other parents through groups and net-
works.

2. Remind yourself that having others help you does not mean
you are an inadequate parent.

3. Advocate for your child's participation in the community by
educating teachers, Jewish leaders, and other professionals.

4. Use your pediatrician as a resource to coordinate services,
interpret data, help make complex responsibilities more manageable, and provide continuity.

Teaching Children to Appreciate Differences

A rainy Sunday afternoon at the mall. You and your three-year-old are rounding the curve, making your approach to the food court, when your daughter finds herself eye-to-knee with a pretty young woman in a wheelchair. "Mommy," she blurts out in a voice loud enough to shake the sprinkles off her yogurt cone, "what is that lady riding in?"

As parents, we have significant influence on shaping the perceptions and attitudes of our children toward people with disabilities. How can we assist them to grow up as sensitive, aware citizens who appreciate the differences among people? How can we help them to live the Jewish ideal of treating with dignity and respect all who are created in God's image?

"A man strikes many coins from one die, and they are all alike," said the rabbis in the Talmud. "But God strikes every person from the die of the first man, yet not one resembles the other. Therefore everyone must say, 'For my sake was the world created!'" (*Sanhedrin* 4:5). Judaism teaches that each person is unique; appreciation of the individual's own special qualities is the foundation for respect from others.

The rabbis even created a special blessing to respond to the experience of encountering a person who looks different. "One who sees a *kushi* [an Ethiopian, i.e. a person with a skin color different from what the rabbis were used to], or people with disfigured faces or limbs, recites the blessing, 'Blessed are You, Lord our God, King of the universe, who makes people different.'" This blessing is also said when seeing a person who was born blind or lame. (*Mishnei Torah, Hilchot B'rachot* 10:12, based on *B'rachot* 58b).

Analyzing this blessing in . . . *Who Makes People Different: Jewish Perspectives on the Disabled*, Rabbi Carl Astor explains it as "an expression of awe and wonder at the great variety of humankind . . . Seeing an individual who is so dramatically different from us gives us the opportunity to appreciate all differences among people." Rabbi Astor also views the blessing as an effort to overturn prejudice against people with disabilities. As reflected in Biblical law, Judaism had a much more enlightened view of people with disabilities than did other contemporaneous cultures. For example, individuals who were blind and deaf were protected from poverty, neglect, and abuse by explicit laws (such as *Leviticus* 19:14).

Today, we are increasingly aware of people with disabilities, and of their right to be fully integrated into the community.

The Americans with Disabilities Act of 1990 requires—among other provisions—the removal of physical barriers which prevent people with disabilities from participating in our communities. But what about psychological barriers? Fortunately, our children do not start out carrying the same emotional baggage about people with disabilities as many adults. It is natural for children to ask questions in unfamiliar situations. When we respond to our children's questions in a straightforward and direct manner, we help them to understand about the world of disabilities in the same matter-of-fact way that they understand about tall people or short people or people who wear glasses. We can help very young children realize that disabilities are not contagious, and that people with disabilities are not dangerous or to be avoided.

The words we use to refer to people who have disabilities are very powerful. When we talk about people being "confined" or "bound" to a wheelchair, or about people who are "victims of cerebral palsy" or "mentally defective," we tell our children that these individuals are to be pitied and that a disability is something to be feared. When we use people-first language instead, words that emphasize the person first and the disability second, we affirm the humanity of those with disabilities and emphasize ways in which they are similar to us. Paul, who has mental retardation, likes to bowl and helps his Mom make challah for Shabbat. Naomi, who is blind, loves rock and roll and is a great dancer.

With the movement toward inclusion, children with disabilities are increasingly being integrated into schools and classrooms. But meanwhile, many of our daughters and sons have not had the opportunity to play and study with their peers who have disabilities.

In *My Special Friend*, a children's book by Floreva G. Cohen, photographs and words tell of the friendship between two boys, one of whom has Down Syndrome, who meet in synagogue each week. Jonathan and Doron become partners in leading the "Adon Olam" prayer at the end of the service. This story demonstrates "how much better [it is] to regard someone primarily as a person *with abilities*, and only secondarily as someone who may need assistance to use those abilities," as presented in "That All May Worship: An Interfaith Welcome to People with Disabilities."[1]

We can seek and create such opportunities for our children to interact with people with disabilities. We can help assure that children with disabilities are welcome and valued participants in our day care centers, playgrounds, and schools. We can advocate with our children's religious and public schools to provide the necessary supports to integrate children who have disabilities into the same classrooms and playing fields as other students. We can encourage the use of disability awareness experiences, such as "Kids on the Block," "Dignity and Disability," or "Justice, Justice for All," which can be incorporated into religious studies for Jewish children in the elementary grades.

And while our children are very sensitive to what we say, they are even more aware of what we do—of the extent to which our behavior reflects the values we espouse. We can include adults who have disabilities in our congregations and community organizations. We can demonstrate to our children that as the teaching "All Israel is responsible for the other" obligates us to assume responsibility for

---

[1]National Organization on Disability, 910 16th St. NW, Suite 600, Washington, DC 20006.

members of our community who may need assistance, we are all enriched by the full citizenship and participation of people with differing abilities, perspectives, and contributions.

Meanwhile, back at the mall, a young mother feels embarrassed. In expressing the curiosity so natural to young children, our three-year-old has put her mother on the spot, and possibly offended the stranger. The woman in the wheelchair smiles. "It's my wheelchair, and this is how I get around. If it's okay with your mother, I'll give you a ride."

"Different" Means "Unique"

1. When children ask questions about people who look different from them, their intention is to get information, not to embarrass adults or to be unkind, says Mary Beth Quinsey, author of the children's book, *Why Does That Man Have Such A Big Nose?* Adults can use children's natural curiosity as a starting point to teach a healthy appreciation of differences.

2. If it is appropriate, answer the child's question immediately and directly. If you wish to delay answering in order to avoid embarrassment, however, tell the child *when* you will do so, and then follow through. Answering a child's question in a matter-of-fact way will give the message that this is not a taboo subject.

3. While we can teach our children not to stare or point, says Quinsey, we also need to let them know that people who look different should not be ignored either.

4. Seek opportunities for your child to get to know individuals with disabilities. This is the best way to develop an appreciation of the unique qualities of each person.

Pulling Together after Coming Apart: Life Cycle Events for Families of Divorce

Adam has just beautifully chanted the Torah reading and Haftorah on his long-awaited Bar Mitzvah day. The rabbi asks Stan and Bonnie to join their son in reciting the *Shehecheyanu* prayer of thanksgiving upon reaching this joyous occasion. Adam's parents, divorced two years ago, rise with full hearts and mixed emotions, reflected in the faces of other family members and friends. Adam is almost overwhelmed by his own feelings at this moment that has brought his parents together with him.

Scenes like this take place in congregations many times each year. There is scarcely a Jewish family that has not been affected by divorce, either personally or through its extended circle of relatives, friends, or colleagues. Between 20% and 33% of American Jewish children today live in households where one or both parents have divorced and remarried, or in single-parent households, according to a 1991 demographic study by Dr. Gary A. Tobin of Brandeis University.

We expect Jewish holidays and life cycle events like Bar and Bat Mitzvahs to be times of family unity, shared pride and joy. However, for families of divorce, these occasions often re-open old wounds for both parents and children. "It never ends," says Ken, a divorced father of three who has remarried. "The children are your connection. First you deal with it at the Bar Mitzvah, then confirmation, graduation, and again at the wedding. You are forced to confront the issues over and over—on birthdays, Mother's and Father's Day, and Jewish holidays like Rosh Hashanah, Yom Kippur, and Passover—all the times when families traditionally gather."

Some of these occasions are public, bringing together both divorced parents and the child, and often stepfamilies as well. Others, such as holidays, are private, requiring that the child be with one or the other parent, whether by legal or parental arrangement, or by the child's own choice once he or she reaches age 18. At the core of all these milestone events is loss. As these occasions accumulate, the child of divorce collects fractured images and memories. For this child, it is much harder to achieve positive family experiences and memories. Even years later, an adult child of divorced parents may relive the trauma of divorce—one at her own marriage, another at the bris of his child.

Planning for public life cycle events, finding the time to accomplish many extra tasks in an already busy schedule, and juggling many people's wishes can create much anxiety and tension even for intact families. But for families of divorce, the planning goes beyond normal stresses. Old anger is fueled and sadness re-awakened. Animosities are aggravated by the need for teamwork when a couple is no longer a team.

Divorced parents face a multitude of dilemmas arousing strong emotions. Whose names should appear on the invitation? Should both sides of the family be invited to the reception, even if they don't get along? Should family members who treated the other spouse insensitively during the divorce now be given special honors? Should stepfamilies be included in the service and reception? Should an ex-spouse who has not paid child support in over a year receive an *aliyah?* The issue of who is paying the bills is particularly troublesome: does that person or family get more decision-making power and more rights? Questions like these tend to immobilize all involved, threatening to overshadow the true joy that should accompany the occasion.

As immersed as parents may be in their own issues, they need to be aware of their child's feelings. Leah felt overwhelmed by the decisions she had to make in preparing for her Bat Mitzvah last year. "I wanted to be involved, but because my parents are divorced," Leah says, "I had twice as many decisions. Then I had to remember to tell each parent what was decided with the other one. Sometimes I felt caught in the middle when my parents couldn't agree. I had to put aside some of my own wishes." Adds Ruth, Leah's mother, "I could see her trying to please both parents when each of us was offering a different opinion. Knowing she is dependent on us and loves us both, I wondered how could she decide whom to please and whom to hurt?"

As a big day like Bar or Bat Mitzvah or confirmation approaches, the nervousness adolescents normally feel is compounded for children of divorce by other anxieties. Will my father, who has had no contact with the family, show up? Will my parents embarrass me by fighting in public? How will all my relatives from different sides of the family get along? Why do I have to have two separate parties?

On the other hand, when divorced parents have an amicable relationship and cooperate in planning an event, the child may have an illusion of family unity, hoping they can get back together. It is important to explain that although the couple can work together on occasion for the child, they cannot work together in the marriage. Parents need to behave in a way that speaks to their separation, finding a balance between being civil to each other and being overly friendly or intimate.

To parents and children of divorce, milestone events are emotional minefields. Successfully negotiating their way through, in the wise words of fourteen-year-old Leah, requires "respecting each other's ideas and not taking it as a personal attack if your child disagrees with your ideas. Children need to be open about their feelings, too. If you don't tell your parents what you want, it won't happen. Both my parents have remarried. I wanted my stepparents' names on the invitation, and they were."

Above all, parents need to recognize that the *simcha* belongs to their child. All planning should be made in the child's best interest. This means working hard to rise above parental differences and issues. And it means asking what is important to the child. Ruth, Leah's mother, says, "Since we had limited financial resources, I asked Leah what elements of the party she cared most about—the menu, party favors, music, her dress. Wanting her to feel she could handle her own responsibilities for her day, I did not nag her about practicing for the service. Although her father did not always cooperate, I tried to give her a sense of ownership of this experience."

Parents do need to be cautious about giving their child too much power in deciding, however. If Jon dislikes Dad's new wife, he may have to agree to inviting her but not giving her a public honor. Parents also should avoid overburdening their children with information that they have no tools to deal with and decisions that are too heavy.

Paying attention to the child's needs is also important when divorced parents observe life cycle events and holidays separately, for the child may feel pulled in several directions. Many divorce decrees do not give children a choice about where they will go for Rosh Hashanah or the Passover seder. Some children find their spiritual experience of the holidays overshadowed by the need to adjust to changed family circumstances. One parent may value religious observance more than the other, for example. Some of these children later opt to stay at college on such occasions, having lost their unified family home and a positive association with the holiday.

Whether families of divorce observe life cycle events together or apart, the vital question for parents to ask is what they can give their child to create positive family experiences and memories.

How Divorced Parents Can Smooth the Way Through Life Cycle Events

1. Remember that your child loves both parents, and avoid putting her in a position of choosing between you.

2. If you have intense feelings of sadness or anger as you plan a life cycle event, don't use your child as a confidant; he is too emotionally involved. Instead, seek the support of family, friends, or professionals, including your rabbi, who may be able to offer helpful guidelines.

3. Make decisions not on legal or emotional criteria, but with your child's best interests in mind.

4. Give your child a sense of control by involving her in planning without making her responsible for the decisions.

5. Be a *mensch*, behaving in a way that models traits you want your child to emulate. You are in charge of you.

The "X" Factor: How Parents' New Relationships after Divorce Affect the Children

Cruising down Main Street, a large, luxurious car sports a license plate announcing "IM HIS X." Cars have long been status symbols, but what would motivate someone to use this vehicle to broadcast her marital status? The message here suggests the ambivalence of many divorced people who are feeling ready for new relationships, but still define themselves in terms of their ex-spouse.

"Divorce is bittersweet," as Sheila Peltz Weinberg was told by her rabbi when it happened to her. Describing her experience as "One Single Jew" in *Jewish Marital Status*, a Hadassah Study edited by Carol Diament, Weinberg says, "One experiences the death of collective life and the birth of a discrete human being." She saw her life as "a maze of contradictions, colliding and birthing changes," and asked, "What can we transmit to our children besides the flexibility to live with change?" Weinberg has found strength and meaning in connections she has forged for herself and her children with the Jewish community and Jewish observance.

When a divorced parent has one foot in the past and the other foot in the future, how are the children affected? Whether anxious or eager about starting a new chapter in their lives, parents may find that carrying over unresolved issues from a past marriage can create problems for their children. These issues frequently surface when a parent begins a new relationship.

Children of divorce are experiencing events that dramatically affect them but that are beyond their control. They feel powerless because they can't reverse the train of events and get their parents back together. Many children wonder if they have contributed to the breakdown of the marriage. Parents can make this transition less painful by helping their children recognize and accept what they can and cannot control.

First, assure your children that it's not their fault. Tell them that adults are in charge of the initial decision to divorce and in charge of whatever will happen now. Consider each child's age and maturity level in deciding how much information to disclose about the reasons for the divorce.

In addition, parents should tell their children honestly that they are not getting back together, and follow up with appropriate behavior. Children are confused when one parent keeps coming back to the house. They are frightened when they hear arguments about matters like finances or custody, making them feel that their parents are not able to take care of them. Issues between divorced parents should be discussed privately.

The legal aspects of divorce can be overwhelming to children. Again, children need to know that adults are in charge here. Rabbi Ervin Preis of Suburban Orthodox Congregation points out that divorce, both civil and religious, severs a legal union between the parents only. According to Jewish law, a Jewish divorce, called a *Get*, is necessary so that both parties can re-marry. Ideally, the legal divorce should not mean the dissolution of the relationship between parents and child.

Getting involved with another adult after divorce can be daunting, partly because of the fear of repeating past mistakes and the difficulty of breaking old patterns. But divorce is an opportunity to learn and grow, to focus on one's strengths as well as on changes one would like to make.

If the adults reach a clear understanding of why the marriage dissolved and what their roles were, they can more successfully undertake new relationships. But they must also reach some emotional closure and resolve feelings of anger, bitterness, and regret. Children feel insecure if they think their parents are falling apart emotionally. Seeking professional help and support for both parents and children can be beneficial. Parents also need to set their goals consciously. As one divorced mother put it, "I can direct most of my energy to finding another husband, or I can live a full life with the possibility that marriage may not be in the picture."

Divorced adults are usually aware that they may differ from their ex-spouses in their readiness for new relationships. As parents, however, they may not realize that their children's readiness is unlikely to coincide with their own. Most children of divorce, at any age, fantasize that their parents will re-unite, long after the parents have separated. When a parent begins to date, children are reminded of the loss of the family unit, and many feel renewed sadness or anger. Some children try to make their parent feel guilty; others withdraw or act up in front of the date.

It is important to pay attention to your child's reactions and understand the causes. When your child is hostile to the new man in your life, is it because, in her mind, *no one* can ever replace her father? Or is your child responding to this individual's personality and the way he treats her? If you wish to continue dating this person, you could try giving him and your child a break from each other, and then slowly re-introduce them. The success of a new relationship may well depend on how much consideration the person you choose shows, not only for your needs, but for your child's.

Many children simply feel ambivalent about this new step by their parent and about how it will affect them. In his first meeting with Devorah, the woman his father had been seeing for several months, ten-year-old Michael showed his anxiety by talking non-stop. Janice, on the other hand, had accepted the fact that her divorced mother was going out, but she was upset when Mom brought home a man she was dating and the visit coincided with her parents' wedding anniversary. Life cycle occasions like birthdays, anniversaries, and Bar or Bat Mitzvahs are especially sensitive times.

Some children actively encourage dating, seeing it as a way to find another adult to bring happiness to a parent who has been depressed and lonely, or to care for the parent so the child can stop worrying. Here is a potential new family, thinks the child; now everything will go back to normal. A danger is that the child may get very attached to this new person and suffer another loss if the relationship ends, or doesn't turn out as he wished.

As a parent, you can help your child accept your new relationship in several ways. First, separate your needs from those of your child. You are entitled to move on with your life. Remember, however, that your child did not choose this person and may not share your feelings for him or her. Give your child time to understand and absorb what is happening. Be aware of your child's feelings, and keep the lines of communication open. Find the right balance between offering too much information and not enough. A new relationship can be an opportunity to model, for children, a different way adults can interact with each other to express gentleness, caring, and love.

Relationships other than romantic ones can fill the deep human needs for companionship, understanding, and shared interests and activities. A good *friend* can greatly enrich one's personal and family life. It may be a friend from your previous married life, or a new one. When children see a parent enjoying the company of another adult, and when they feel included in that relationship, they can relax and reap the benefits of warmth and caring extended to them. "One of the joys of a Jewish community that celebrates together [such as a *chavurah*]," writes Sheila Peltz Weinberg, "is the opportunity for children to develop independent relationships with other adults. . . . Occasionally, my children connect with people that I don't particularly find appealing, but who have the quality that meets the children in their world. This is a blessing, especially for a single parent. . . ."

Most of all, reassure your child with the message, "I may be HIS or HER X, but I will always be your parent, and you will always be my child."

Suggestions for Divorced Parents in New Relationships

1. Avoid setting up conflicts of loyalty for your children. Respect their privacy by refraining from asking them about your ex-spouse's new relationships.

2. Consider the seriousness of the new relationship before introducing your child to a person with whom you are involved.

3. Find common interests between your child and the new person in your life. Plan some activities away from home on neutral turf so that they can get acquainted.

4. Avoid pointing out to your children comparisons and contrasts between your ex-spouse and your new relationship.

5. Make special time alone with your children, particularly if you are a non-custodial parent. Observing Shabbat and Jewish holidays together, when possible, strengthens the sense of belonging to your family and the Jewish community.

Stresses and Strains

Fears about School

Since beginning first grade, Michael had complained of a stomach ache every Sunday night. Normally a sound sleeper, he started awakening with bad dreams. By Monday morning, he was nauseated and had a headache. Finding their son had no fever, Jon and Paula sent him to school. After a few weeks they began to notice a pattern, with Michael's symptoms appearing on Sundays and Mondays, and gradually diminishing as the week went on until they disappeared entirely on the weekends.

Michael's ills were real, but their cause was not physical. Rather, they were due to his apprehension about going to school. Many children are fearful of moving into the unknown, whether it be situations such as a new school or a different grade, or new relationships that may or may not work out. Such fears typically surface at or shortly after the beginning of the school year.

Among younger children between the ages of 2 and 3, a stage of separation anxiety is normal when they leave family and familiar circumstances, says Sandee Lever, director of the Goldsmith Early Childhood Education Center of Chizuk Amuno Congregation. "A child this age fears an unknown situation and especially fears that Mommy won't come back," Lever continues. She points out that these are natural reactions, and most children adapt within a month. Lever emphasizes that "It is very important for the school to build trust in the parents so that they realize their child is cared for by warm, nurturing teachers who are experienced in dealing with children's reactions to separation." Children who have been affected by actual losses, through death or divorce, for example, understandably may have more difficulty with separation anxiety.

Children's fears about school take different forms at different ages, but the underlying question at almost all ages seems to be "Am I O.K.?" Fears have to do with finding out that maybe "I am not O.K." There are many common fears among children. "Am I going to fail?" "Will I know where things are?" "Who will I be sitting next to?" "Will I do as well this year as I did last year?" "Am I going to look like a dummy?" "Am I going to feel like a dummy?" "Are people going to tease me?" "Will I have friends?"

Some children can articulate their fears to their parents and ask for help in dealing with them. But many parents first become aware of a problem through changes in behavior, such as Michael's. Major warning signs are changes in eating or sleeping habits, and any behavior that is different from the child's normal pattern. For example, if a child is usually energetic and active but suddenly becomes lethargic, that is a signal. Increased whining and irritability, or reverting to behavior typical of a younger age such as kicking, biting, or screaming, are also signs that something is bothering the child.

At the same time that children are dealing with their fears about school, parents too are worrying, "Will my child be O.K.?" Parents may share some of their children's fears connected to adjusting to a new situation, such as making friends or being teased because of their appearance or athletic ability. Other worries of parents are: "Will he get hurt?," "Will she be able to cope?," and "Will he live up to his potential, or will he somehow disappoint himself or his family?" Parents wonder about whether their children will have minds of their own, be leaders or followers, get into trouble, and be able to stand up for what they believe in. The pre-adolescent and adolescent years bring fears about involvement with drugs and alcohol, and about sexuality. Some anxieties are intensified today because of issues of personal physical safety in an increasingly dangerous world.

When students are being educated at a Jewish day or Hebrew school, other parental fears may arise. "Will our child develop a different religious commitment that may make us feel uncomfortable?" "Are we going to be able to help our child in his/her Judaic studies in the same way that we can offer support for general studies?" "How can we keep track of what our child is learning in Hebrew if we can't read or speak the language?"

Underlying many of these fears for the child are parents' concerns about whether or not they have done a "good enough" job. Many parents think that their child's adjustment and acceptance reflect parental success or failure. This concern may be communicated to the child as pressure to live up to the parents' expectations. Jane E. Brody, in a *New York Times* article titled, "Averting a Crisis from School Phobia," points out that some children are so afraid of failing—and especially of falling short of their parents' expectations—that "their very fear often becomes a self-fulfilling prophecy."[1]

When Michael's parents talked with him and his teacher, they found that Michael's anxieties about entering a new grade and making friends were exacerbated by the fact that several of his classmates arrived in first grade able to read. Michael realized that his parents were disappointed that he was not yet reading, and he felt inadequate. The teacher helped Jon and Paula ease up on the pressure they were putting on their son, so that he felt free to develop at his own pace and enjoy his new school experience. Within a few weeks, Michael's physical symptoms had disappeared.

Dr. Baron D. Schmitt, a pediatrician at the Children's Hospital in Denver, Colorado and author of *Your Child's Health*, advises parents to make going to school a "non-negotiable activity" when a child is developmentally ready to handle separation (usually by first grade).[2] If there are physical symptoms of anxiety, you should alert the teacher and the school nurse.

As your child matures, help her develop ways to deal with the situations that arise in her life rather than trying to handle challenges for her. Distinguish between your fears as a parent and your child's fears. A child needs to be allowed to experience fear and then to let go of it in order to develop. Help your child anticipate problems and work out strategies for coping with them.

---

[1] Jane E. Brody, "Averting a Crisis from School Phobia," *New York Times*, September 4, 1991.

[2] *Ibid.*

Although children have always had fears and parents have had fears for their children, we are increasingly affected by the culture around us. The mass media, with their pervasive influence, tend to celebrate external accomplishments and emphasize "fitting in," instead of encouraging us to turn to our own values to decide what we feel is important. For instance, parents may worry more about whether their children will get high grades than about how they feel about themselves or whether they are *menschen*—good people.

A song often taught to young children in Hebrew and day schools is based on the teaching in *Pirke Avot* (*Ethics of the Fathers*, 1:2) that "The world is sustained on three pillars: Torah, worship, and acts of lovingkindness." The Talmud states, "Whoever does deeds of charity and justice is considered as having filled the world with lovingkindness." (Sukkah 49b.) If parents and educators together promote these Jewish values, they can make school a very positive experience for children.

The most important thing parents can do is to give their children every opportunity to feel good about themselves. This creates self-esteem, the basis of self-confidence. And self-confidence allows one to take risks and to cope with the challenges that life presents.

Suggestions for Enhancing a Child's Adjustment to School

1. Be aware of warning signs that your child may be struggling with a problem, and help him put it into words. Find some quiet moments for yourself each day so you are refreshed enough to be available to your child when he needs you.

2. Prepare for a new situation. When your child is entering a new school, visit the school together and meet the teachers before the first full day. A very young child can take along a familiar toy or family photo. Arrange for your child to meet a few classmates before the year begins. Read library books together about similar new situations. Make a personalized book with your child, such as "Michael's New School," to make the unknown more familiar.

3. Learn along with your child. If you have a limited background in Judaic studies or little knowledge of Hebrew, but you've enrolled your child in a Jewish day school or Hebrew school, obviously Jew-

ish education is important to you. Take a Hebrew conversation class or an adult education course at your synagogue or local university. Many congregations are now offering family education programs where children and parents learn side by side.

4. Be aware of differences between what you want or need and what your child wants or needs. Keep in mind your child's own personality, developmental level, and learning style.

When Your Child Doesn't Fit In

Most of us have known a young child like one of these. Sam speaks too loudly and laughs at inappropriate times. Michael says embarrassing things, and Ricky is the last to be chosen for a team. Ruth dresses differently from other children, and painfully shy Carol doesn't get calls and invitations from classmates. These children often seem unable to hear some of the messages other children and adults are giving. They have trouble understanding the subtle, nonverbal communication on which much of our social interaction relies.

In school and in the neighborhood, these "different" children often experience rejection by their peers, who are quick to label them weird, odd, or worse. Such children may be subjected to ostracism, teasing, ridicule, and even physical harassment.

Carol wonders why she has no friends and why she isn't included in group games. Feeling increasingly bad about herself, unable to express these feelings even to her parents, she retreats into a shell, telling herself, "I don't need others." Michael, on the other hand, assumes the role of class clown, while Sam starts bullying others, preferring negative attention to none at all.

While these kinds of behavior usually become apparent in school and in the neighborhood, they are often mirrored in the ways such children relate to their siblings and parents. Frequently, however, it is a teacher who first brings the behavior to the parents' attention. Parents may not realize the extent of the problem, or may ask whether the school is doing its job. Others feel they have overlooked or minimized signs of their child's unhappiness, reacting with guilt. Whatever their response, these parents hurt for their children, for they want them to fit in and feel good about themselves. And parents want to know *why* their children are different.

Extreme shyness or a lack of social skills in children may have many causes. Usually there is a genetic component. The behavior is sometimes connected to a learning disability or to attention deficit disorder. The problem may also be a temporary response to a family crisis such as the separation or divorce of parents, the death of a loved one, or a move to another city. Frequently several of these factors combine to create a more complex situation.

Dr. Stanley Greenspan, author of *First Feelings,* notes that, although children seem to have basic personality characteristics right from birth, parents can foster healthy growth by understanding the emotional milestones children experience starting in infancy. Dr. Greenspan urges parents to trust their intuition. If, for example, parents have an uneasy sense that their infant seems "different," he advises taking constructive action early instead of "waiting passively for confirmation of their assessment from an alert teacher or some other outside authority."

In addition, an awareness of the normal developmental and behavioral stages that young children pass through will help parents develop realistic expectations for their children, says Vivian Chait, director of a Jewish Community Center pre-school/kindergarten program. "Worrying because your child is not playing cooperatively at age 2 is not a developmentally appropriate expectation. However, if your child does not want to be touched, is biting others, or just does not seem happy, these are signs of a problem," she explains.

Rabbi Mendel Freedman, principal of the Bais Yaakov School for Girls Elementary School, stresses respecting the child's individual personality. A very sociable parent may worry unnecessarily about her shy child when the shyness is not actually causing problems with peers. Rabbi Freedman also advises looking at the social context. "If your child is not getting invitations from classmates, it may not mean she is being excluded; inviting friends home is more important to some groups than to others."

Once parents identify a problem that is affecting their child's happiness and social interaction, what can they do to help? Underlying all efforts should be the goal of building the child's self-esteem and confidence. Ben and Laura describe their daughter Carol in the early grades as repeatedly opting to be in situations where she wouldn't attract attention. For example, she avoided making eye contact with the teacher because she was so afraid of being called on in class. A counselor suggested they find some activity Carol loved and encourage her competence in that. Carol had requested violin lessons. "When we saw she had musical aptitude, we were thrilled," says Ben. "This is something Carol can do well, and it has helped her feel good about herself. Best of all, through the school orchestra, we have been able to use music to open the door to a new social outlet for Carol."

Communication between parent and child is vital. If a problem surfaces at school, acknowledge the problem with your child and let him know that you are here to help make changes so that things can work better. Rabbi Freedman emphasizes the need for special, private time between parent and child, and suggests using more of that time to discuss topics of mutual interest, such as a book read for pleasure, rather than school problems or household tasks.

Use your home as a kind of laboratory to help your child practice appropriate behavior for social situations. Gently point out to him a better way to deal with a specific situation as it arises within the family. For example, help him learn to ask for a toy instead of grabbing it from a sibling. Avoid blaming or punitive responses, pointing out the positive instead.

For the child who is socially ill at ease, parents can arrange situations offering positive social experiences with peers. Invite another child to your home to play, but don't assume the children will do it on their own. With a shy child, you may need to initiate a structured activity like a game, or let the children help you bake cookies. Your role as parent should be that of a guide or facilitator; try to step back and let the children play without directing them too much.

Communication between parents and school is essential. Establish a good rapport with the teachers, and enlist their help in working with your child, as an individual and as a member of the class. Marilyn Levy, general studies supervisor, and Liora Rosen, Hebrew studies supervisor at Bais Yaakov School for Girls, describe several effective approaches teachers can take to help the child who has difficulty socializing feel more comfortable and confident. These include establishing a special rapport based on non-academic subjects of conversation, using reassuring physical contact, orchestrating inclusion of the child in group activities, and providing structured activities during free play time. Other strategies include pairing a child with a good learning buddy, and choosing the child for classroom jobs that involve interaction or visibility, such as handing out papers or holding the flag. Simply seating a shy child in the front of the room will make her feel as if she is more a part of the class. Teachers can also recommend to parents another child who would be a compatible, caring friend.

Other techniques used in some Jewish elementary schools to build individual self-esteem and mutual respect among students include recognition of children's birthdays and "mensch" awards for behavior demonstrating Jewish values, such as going out of one's way to help a fellow student. Giving every child in a class a turn at being "Student of the Week," regardless of academic or behavioral merit, allows teachers to elicit from the child's classmates positive comments about qualities they like and admire in that individual. These approaches can be adapted for secular schools as well.

When a child is demonstrating disruptive and aggressive verbal or physical behavior, parents and teachers can plan a behavior modification program that will ensure consistency at home and in school. While acknowledging the child's feelings, it is important to set limits and control his energies. Using rewards—such as stickers, an extra story at bedtime, or a special toy or excursion the child wants—can encourage acceptable behavior.

If none of these approaches is working and problems persist, parents can seek professional help from their pediatrician, the school guidance counselor, a social worker, psychologist, or family counselor. With these resources, often the situation can significantly improve within months.

Judaism provides an enlightening model for the family with a child "who doesn't fit in." The name "Yisrael" has been seen by rabbinic commentators as an acronym for the 600,000 Hebrew men who left Egypt (Exodus 12:37). This is significant because "no individual can keep the entire Torah. Only when each member of Yisrael contributes his or her unique abilities and traits can all the commandments be fulfilled," explains psychologist Aviva Weisbord. At Sinai, preparing to receive the Ten Commandments, "All the people answered together [as one], saying 'All that the Lord has spoken, we will do.'" (Exodus 19:8) This text emphasizes the fact that everyone counts and each person, including each child, has innate value and a role to play, says Dr. Weisbord. Conveying this central message of Judaism can build a child's feelings of importance and strength.

It takes many small steps to build a child's confidence, and one successful experience leads to another. Parents play an essential role in this gradual process by giving their child the benefits of their patience, love, encouragement, and support.

Suggestions for Easing a Child's Social Interaction

1. Give your child small life experiences to build confidence, such as helping her learn to order her own meal in a restaurant.

2. You know your child best. Listen to your intuition. Seek the help of school staff and other professionals if you sense your child is "different" in some way that is making him unhappy or interfering with his social adjustment.

3. Attend parenting workshops, programs, or support groups, and read to learn about child development.

4. Advocate for your child by maintaining good communication with the school and by helping her learn social skills at home.

Are We Overprogramming Our Children?

It's 7:15 on a Thursday night. After a full school day in which she took two tests and played in an intramural soccer game, Linda came home from Hebrew school and ate a quick dinner. Now she sits down to start her homework. Fifteen minutes later, Mom finds Linda asleep over her books.

Is it any wonder this child is exhausted? At age ten, her regular after-school and weekend pursuits include gymnastics, piano lessons, and Girl Scouts, as well as Hebrew studies. Linda's mother, who works part-time, laughingly calls her typical day "schlep and drop." But does she realize what price her child and the whole family are paying for Linda's busy life?

Children who are involved in too many structured extra activities have no wind-down time left, no time just to be and to develop their own inner resources. The entire family loses when the individual child's outside activities leave no time for all to enjoy together. And a frazzled parent who goes straight from work to carpool to making dinner creates tension felt by everyone at home.

How can you tell if your child is overprogrammed? First, you need to know your own child's needs, interests, abilities, and energy level. Is he showing more fatigue than usual? Is she objecting to dance class, which she used to love? Some children show resistance indirectly, through misbehavior or increased clinginess, says psychologist Dr. Aviva Weisbord. "I don't want to go to ballet" may really mean "I want some time with and attention from my parents."

It is important for parents to examine their motives for filling their children's schedules. Working parents may be seeking a solution for the problem of finding coverage for children after school. Others are motivated by social pressure. Says Alan, father of two, "All the kids in our neighborhood are in Little League. I want my boys to be part of the group."

Dr. Weisbord sees today's parents as different from post-Depression parents, who tried to give their children material things that they themselves had lacked. "This generation has a tremendous fear of missing out on any opportunity for the child's development," Dr. Weisbord observes. She attributes the pressure parents feel to the way the media bombard us with information from experts on child development.

Parents usually view extra activities as opportunities for their children to enjoy, acquire new skills, and learn useful lessons such as sharing, discipline, or being a team player. They hope to see their children achieve something that will make them all proud. These are positive, valid goals. But if a child is resisting, it may be a signal that the parent's need for the child to achieve has superseded the child's own needs and desires.

To avoid overprogramming, approach your child as an individual, determining the pace that is best for him or her. Avoid comparisons with other children, including siblings. Consider the child's age. With a young child, who is more pliable and open to parents' influence, look at the developmental level. Does your son have enough skill and concentration to succeed at piano? Or are you setting him up for disappointment and frustration that might make him unwilling to try an instrument again later? Remember that he will grow and change.

"Living as Jews in a diaspora society, we are constantly faced with conflicting demands on our time," says Rachel Glaser, Educational Director of Beth Israel Hebrew School. When these conflicts directly involve our life as Jews, then we have to make choices. As parents, how can we resolve with our children such dilemmas as choosing soccer league games or Hebrew school, art class or synagogue attendance, going out with friends or being home with the family on Friday night, and going to school or staying out to observe a Jewish holiday?

Each family needs to decide what Jewish values and observances it wishes to emphasize. Rachel Glaser urges parents to ask themselves: Is it important for our child to learn how to live as a Jew? If this is a goal, then you will need to support your child's Jewish education. If you feel Judaism is an important part of your family's life, now and for the future, says Mrs. Glaser, you can give your child clear instead of ambivalent messages, and support his or her growing Jewish identity.

Assess your family's priorities. If Shabbat observance is important, for example, find a sports league that plays only on weekdays. Look for courses or programs offering the flexibility of a make-up class if there is a conflict with a Jewish holiday. Let your child know what matters to you, and avoid creating an either/or conflict that he is left to resolve. You may need to advocate for your child, speaking to coaches or teachers. "Ben will be 10 minutes late for basketball practice on Tuesdays because he'll be coming from Hebrew School. That's important to our family." Hearing this, Ben understands that he can balance the commitments in his life without diminishing either his enjoyment of sports or his family's values.

While students attending Jewish day schools do not encounter as many conflicts as those in Hebrew school programs, day school students still face many options, says Leslie Smith Rosen, Middle School Head at Krieger Schechter Day School. Mrs. Rosen points out that one benefit of observing Shabbat—for *any* Jewish family—is that the unscheduled time offers rich opportunities for family interaction, as well as for children to explore and develop their own inner resources.

In deciding on your family's priorities, include your child in making decisions. Too many options for extra activities can be overwhelming. With a young child, you can select a few from which she can choose.

Older children can more clearly identify their interests and are more influenced by peers in making choices. Rachel Glaser recommends that parents not simply impose a rule, but talk with their children about what's important *ahead of time*, before issues arise. Bar or Bat Mitzvah is an ideal time to discuss what continued and new Jewish commitments your child wants to make, and how you feel about that. "When older children are given a voice about how to manage the Jewish part of their lives, they feel respected and they are generally responsive," observes Glaser. It is up to adults to find ways to involve them, and to give them responsibilities, in home life, in the synagogue, and in the Jewish community.

What happens when an extra-curricular pastime—whether initiated originally by the parents or by the child—does not work out and the child wants to drop it? If the child was not developmentally ready or simply did not enjoy the activity, she should not be made to feel she has failed. Problems often arise over the money invested. Blaming the child for the dollars "wasted" is not helpful. It is beneficial for parents to understand beforehand that any activity may not work out as they and their child had hoped. Are you able and willing to forfeit some money? If not, then make a smaller scale, alternative plan. Before buying a karate uniform, for example, try a few sample classes. You will pay a higher price if you keep a child in an activity against his will.

If parents think carefully about their expectations of their child and the family's priorities, they can avoid pushing too much. Instead, they can encourage and foster their child's growth through selected activities in a manageable schedule.

Suggestions for Relaxing the Schedule Crunch

1. Negotiate a short time-span with a child for trying a new activity, whether the original impetus comes from parent or child. Let the child know you will all have a chance to evaluate how it's going after a given period of time, such as six months.

2. Look for opportunities to combine interests and priorities, such as a Jewish basketball team or musical group.

3. Find an activity in which parent and child can participate together. Be a team coach or a scout leader. Even simply being there as a spectator while your child's team plays shows that you care.

4. Leave time for family recreation. Don't forget the simple pleasures of just being together. Take a walk or a bike ride, play in the yard, sit on the porch and read a story or talk. Set aside some unstructured time, such as on Shabbat afternoon, on a regular basis, to relax together. Give your child experiences that reflect your own happy memories of family in a less hectic time.

Dealing with Rejection

Spring semester of senior year: your child has worked and waited a long time to reach this point. In addition to meeting academic and extra-curricular commitments at school, he or she has spent countless hours researching colleges, making choices, visiting campuses, writing essays, and filling out applications. You've all worried and dreamed. Finally, the results are in. The bad news is that some of your child's—and your own—highest hopes have crashed.

Rejection hurts. It's natural, at a time like this, for both parent and child to feel disappointment, sadness, and even anger. "It's not fair!" you want to shout—and you're right. The college admission process is subjective, the competition largely invisible, and a wide range of factors considered, points out Alice Margraff, a college counselor at McDonogh School in McDonogh, Maryland. Who is accepted by which schools is a reflection of the applicant pool that year, says Jeannie Ginsberg, College Guidance Counselor at Beth Tfiloh Community Day School. The hard truth is that the student does not have control over a good part of the process.

If the post office has delivered some thin envelopes instead of fat ones, you can help your child deal with the aftermath. First, he or she needs to allow time to acknowledge feelings such as sadness or anger. Rejection does create dejection. But life isn't always fair—and this experience can become an opportunity to learn how to face some of the disappointments life may later bring.

Disappointment results from measuring outcomes against expectations. College counselors generally encourage high school students to "reach" by applying to one or two challenging schools. Mental preparation for possible let-downs is part of that process— "nothing ventured, nothing gained." What works best is combining a sense of optimism with a realistic approach and developing a balanced set of options, says Elizabeth Ottinger, Director of College Counseling at McDonogh School. Through research and preparation, students undertake a kind of personal search. "The goal," says Ottinger, "is not to find the one perfect school, but to find the best match for one's talents and interests. Through the process, one does a lot of growing."

And part of growing up is learning to deal with disappointments. Tell your child: "If you think about it, you have already accumulated some experience with rejection. Perhaps you tried out for the football team or the cheerleading squad, and didn't make it. How did it feel when you weren't chosen for that part you really wanted in the school play, or when you just missed making the honor roll? Maybe you've felt the sting of rejection after a meaningful relationship with a girlfriend or boyfriend. You picked yourself up and learned from these losses. Now you can use those coping skills to help you over this rough time. Give yourself credit for, and draw on, your own strengths. This experience, one step on the road to adulthood, can also help prepare you for future challenges, such as applying for a job.

"Above all, remember that acceptance or rejection by a college is not a reflection of who you are. Where you go to college is not the measure of how successful you'll be in life." The Jewish community has traditionally prized education, but the most important keys to our identity are our *values*, not our academic achievements.

"Easy to say," your child may be thinking, "but how am I going to face Mom and Dad, Grandma and Grandpa, or that special teacher who really wanted me to go to this college?" Indeed, your child may be feeling that he has let others down. Your reaction to his disappointment is going to have a big impact. Be sensitive and understanding. Remember that this is *his* life, and help him focus on his own values, needs, and goals. When the college process has worked well, says Elizabeth Ottinger, parents and their children have come to know each other better by clarifying what is important to each of them, and some compromises may already have been reached. Allow your child to use this opportunity to communicate about what matters most to him.

Reactions from peers may also be difficult to deal with. An awkward situation evoking mixed emotions sometimes results when good friends or rivals apply to the same school and only one is accepted. It is hard for an adolescent not to be affected by classmates who have assured her that "you'll get in" or who have strong opinions about which schools are most prestigious. Urge your child to keep her own goals in mind. Ottinger also advises discretion: she is not obliged to tell everyone where she was accepted or rejected, just as her SAT scores are her own business. This is a time to draw on the support of friends. Remind your child that good friends value her for who she is, not for what colleges have accepted her.

Though it may seem hard, help your graduate to try thinking beyond *now.* Clichés like "life goes on" and "things will work out for the best" do contain truth. Tell him, "Maybe the school that rejected you was not the best match. Isn't it better to be at a school that wants *you?* College is a new world, and you will change as a result of your time there."

A positive outlook is fundamental, say college counselors. They offer some suggestions about how to cultivate optimism and prepare for the transition to college. First, your child should look at his options and review his reasons for applying to these schools. Once he reaches a decision, you can help him seek reasons he can feel enthusiastic about that college.

It's a good idea to visit the campus and make personal contacts. The campus Hillel director will gladly introduce your son or daughter to undergraduates, who can offer a warm welcome. Hillel offers a built-in community that can become a home away from home, and a connection to Jewish activities and values that can give your adolescent solid footing during what can be a rocky voyage through college. Remember that the college years provide an important opportunity to strengthen the Jewish identity and commitment of your child. The Jewish experiences and Jewish friends young people have during college can significantly influence the kind of Jews they will become as adults.

The high school counselor can provide names of graduates of your child's high school who now attend his college. Chances are that some of them also experienced rejections, and some began freshman year with the idea of trying to transfer out later. But probably, most decided to make the best of it, adjusting well and happy to be where they landed.

Occasionally, a student has no college acceptances. In such a case, all is not lost. Many colleges accept applications over the summer. The high school counselor can help the student through this process. Another option is to wait a year, take courses and/or work, and reapply to find a more suitable match.

"The quality of your life at college is as important as the academic education you get," says Jeannie Ginsberg of Beth Tfiloh. Ideally, says McDonogh's Elizabeth Ottinger, students, parents, and high schools share the same goal: "We want the student to be happy, appropriately challenged, successful, and able to enjoy the entire college experience."

In the process of being judged in competition with others, perhaps your child has had some let-downs. The messages that a parent can give a child at this time are: Graduation is an important turning point, an opportunity to take pride in your past accomplishments. To keep your balance, turn to your values, goals, and sources of emotional support. Use this opportunity to learn to accept rejections or losses and move on. Life is not a one-way street. Perhaps the route you are on is not the one you had in mind, but it may turn out to take you closer to your goals.

Suggestions for Parents of College-Bound Students

1. Beginning in junior year, work with your child and his or her college counselor to develop a balanced group of college options and to set realistic goals.

2. Listen to your child's expressed wishes and priorities in selecting schools. Distinguish his or her needs and desires from your own.

3. When looking at colleges, seriously consider the quality of Jewish life on campus. Discuss with your child what level of Jewish activity will meet his or her needs. Important questions to consider include: Are there enough Jewish students on campus to support a

vibrant Jewish community? Is there an active Hillel organization? Is kosher food readily available? Are Jewish studies courses offered?

4. If your child experiences rejection, offer understanding and support. Help him or her view this as an opportunity for growth. With your encouragement, your child can embark with enthusiasm and make a good adjustment to college.

When Parenting Feels Like an Overwhelming Job

It's 5:30 p.m. Sharon is trying to get dinner on for her four kids. Jason and Scott, ages 8 and 6, are battling over who gets to watch his favorite TV show. Eleven-year-old Janie is in tears because she failed a math test today. The baby is screaming for his bottle. At the height of the bedlam, Sharon's husband Eric calls to say he's been delayed at work.

By 6:00 Sharon has calmed everyone down and dinner is on the table. Suddenly, as he's reaching for the mashed potatoes, Scott knocks over his glass of milk. Sharon explodes. She jumps up, shakes Scott hard, and yells in his face, "You clumsy idiot!" The other children freeze.

Many parents can identify with this scene. We would like home to be a peaceful place, a safety net, but it doesn't always meet that expectation. The truth is that parenting is a challenge. We often feel unprepared and inadequate, as we confront situations we have not encountered before. At times we feel frustrated and at the end of our rope. When we lose control, we may lash out at our children.

"Even well-intentioned parents are at risk due to the stresses of their environment," says Rabbi Joel Mishkin of Temple Beth Shalom in Sarasota, Florida. He points to Biblical parents such as Laban or Lot. While their treatment of their daughters left much to be desired, it should be examined in the social context of their times.

Joan Grayson Cohen, a lawyer and social worker who coordinates the Child Abuse and Neglect Prevention Project of Jewish Family Services, emphasizes that maltreatment of children by parents occurs throughout our society, regardless of economic status, race, and religious affiliation. The Jewish community is not immune.

What triggers a parent's loss of control with a child? Sometimes it is an innocent act or mistake by the child. The proverbial last straw can be as trivial as a lost mitten or spilt milk. When a parent has an excessive reaction—whether it is yelling or using physical force such as shaking, shoving, or hitting—he or she is expressing anger at feeling out of control, often about something that has nothing to do with the child. Or the parent may react by saying, "I can't cope," withdrawing emotionally or actually walking out.

After exploding at a child, the parent may first feel shock: "Did I really do that?" There is also guilt, and a desire to check that the child is O.K. The tendency then is to push the incident under: "This is never going to happen again. I'll control myself next time." It is instead important to pay attention to the incident. The more a parent feels the need to push it away, the greater the chance such outbreaks could recur, with intensified seriousness.

So one needs to ask, "What else is going on that I got so upset? Are there things in my life that I'm worried or angry about, or that I want to change? Where am I feeling frustrated: in my job, marriage, family responsibilities?"

What's happening in Sharon's life that causes her to jump on Scott? Her husband is working longer hours because he is in danger of losing his job. Sharon feels overburdened by her expectations of herself and the demands of child rearing. Though she willingly chose to be at home rather than continue working at her career, she is beginning to feel limited, and she misses professional stimulation. She is not sure her husband would understand her feelings. Instead of blaming or feeling guilty about exploding at her son, Sharon could view this incident as a signal to deal with her situation before it worsens.

Children do sometimes behave in ways that parents perceive as deliberately provoking or uncooperative. A seven-year-old whose mother asks him to play with his three-year-old sister hits her with a wood block. A youngster takes something from Dad's desk without asking his permission, or breaks a possession that had special meaning to Mom. A parent's angry reaction to such incidents is natural, and it is important to help children learn that their behavior has consequences. At the same time, the parent needs to look beyond the behavior to understand the *reasons* for it. What may the child be trying to communicate? Is she really saying, "I need attention that I'm not getting," "This job is too big for me," "I'm afraid because you and Dad are fighting," or "I'm unhappy with myself so I'm going to make you unhappy with me, too"?

In such situations, separate what the child *does* from who the child *is*. It is reasonable to let your child know you're upset at his behavior ("Hitting your sister is not acceptable" or "I'm really angry that you broke the Shabbat tray Grandma gave me"). But telling the child "*You* are bad" because of what he did is a very different message.

As we can learn to distinguish our children's selves from their acts, we also can learn to separate our children from ourselves. Children at times represent that part of us that is most dependent and vulnerable. When they mess up or are whiny and cranky, their behavior touches off our own feelings of inadequacy. We forget that as children, we learned how to do things by trial and error—and that meant making mistakes.

We need to ask if our expectations for our children are reasonable. Is a father who demands that his son get all A's trying to compensate, through his child, for his own disappointing academic performance years ago? Viewing our children as extensions of ourselves, and their deficiencies as reflections of our own failings, interferes with our ability to value them for their unique capabilities.

We may hurt our children in other ways. Children suffer when they are repeatedly ridiculed, demeaned, or criticized, according to a publication by Ohel Children's Home and Family Services prepared with several Orthodox organizations and schools in New York. Name-calling and remarks such as "You're no good," "I wish you'd never been born," or "How can you be so stupid?" wound a child's self-esteem, sense of mastery over his world, and feelings of security. Consider the messages we give children by thoughtless threats like "Stop that whining, you little brat," or "I'm going to kill you if you do that one more time." Listening to some parents talking to their children during a walk through any food market or toy store will reveal the pervasiveness of verbal abuse, both unwitting and intentional. The emotional scars last long beyond childhood.

Parenting is learned. Our most vivid models are our own parents. If we feel they erred and we want to do it differently, we must learn how. Important questions to ask are: How did my parents encourage my self-esteem, my self-confidence, my independence, and my ability to learn and master a task? Did they give me permission to make mistakes? Did they give me the capacity to offer and receive help, share with others, cope with frustration, and express my feelings? Did they let me know I am lovable and can love in return, and that I have something of worth to contribute to others? If so, how did they communicate all that to me?

How we were parented cannot be changed, but how we parent can. When our own adult needs are not being met, when we are feeling overstressed and out of control, we need to separate our needs from those of our children, and seek alternative ways to nurture ourselves. We can turn to our Jewish communal institutions which are committed to strengthening families, including synagogues, Jewish Family Services, and Jewish Community Centers.

Rabbi Harold Schulweis suggests that we accompany the fifth commandment, "Honor thy father and thy mother," with another: "Honor thy son and thy daughter." Respect (literally, "to look again"), says Schulweis, "means to recognize the talents of character which cannot be measured by gold stars and grades. Respect means to recognize the inviolable uniqueness in the other."[1] This is a valuable message for all parents.

Suggestions for Handling Stress

1. When life feels overwhelming, seek professional help, such as marital counseling, individual or family therapy, or rabbinic counseling.

---

[1]Rabbi Harold M. Schulweis, "Honor Thy Son and Thy Daughter," *Baltimore Jewish Times*, and *In God's Mirror: Reflections and Essays*, Hoboken, NJ: KTAV Publishing House, Inc., 1990.

2. Take a class on parenting techniques, child development, or stress management. Many Jewish Family Services and Jewish Community Centers offer such classes or workshops.

3. Join a parents' support group through your synagogue, your child's school, Jewish Family Service, Child Study Association, or Parents Anonymous, or start one with friends.

4. Find ways to get some respite from the demands of parenting. Organize a baby-sitting cooperative. Give yourself some time off periodically to renew yourself.

The Art of Positive Discipline

"I can't control my kids. They have no respect for my authority." "I've tried every punishment under the sun, and nothing works." "I have so little time with my child that I hate to spoil it by conflicts over discipline."

Can you relate to any of these parents? Many of us find parenting a very difficult and stressful job. At times we all feel frustrated, unsure of ourselves, and inadequate. Our task seems all the more overwhelming as we look around and see a general breakdown of discipline in every area of society, from the schools to the military to the law enforcement system. Parents may very well ask, how can we teach our children discipline when they see so many examples of disrespect for rules and failure to take responsibility for one's actions?

At times it may seem that everyone is out of control, but as parents we can still counter negative influences and effect changes in our own homes. This chapter presents the concept of positive discipline as a way we can parent effectively, and discusses some discipline methods that are not effective. The following chapter suggests specific guidelines and techniques that parents can use with children of various ages, from toddlers to teens—the "how to's" of positive discipline.

As parents, we want to give our children the message that they are loved, and we want to raise them to have good self-esteem. We also want to teach them problem-solving and communication skills for life, so that they will be happy, healthy, and productive adults. The main responsibility of parents is to guide our children in developing values and in choosing right from wrong, and discipline is an essential part of that guidance, says Rabbi Hayim Halevy Donin in *To Raise a Jewish Child: A Guide for Parents.*

Discipline helps children develop self-control by setting limits and correcting misbehavior, as defined by Marilyn E. Gootman in "How to Teach Your Children Discipline," a publication of the National Committee for Prevention of Child Abuse. "Discipline also is encouraging children, guiding them, helping them feel good about themselves and their choices, and teaching them how to think for themselves," she says. Discipline is not the same as punishment. Gootman's definition is significant because of its *positive* emphasis on what we can empower our children to do for themselves.

Many parents today, however, do not give their children consistent discipline. One reason is that discipline takes hard work and persistence because children do not learn to change their behavior overnight. Some parents feel guilty that their work schedules require them to be away from their families so much. To compensate, they try to make their time with their children pleasant by avoiding issues of rules and authority. And some parents fear their child will think they are "mean"; setting limits feels less important than having their child *like* them.

Our rabbis centuries ago were aware that parents have these kinds of feelings. Many of the challenges of child-rearing today are the same ones our Biblical forebears faced. Think of the disastrous results of Jacob's favoritism and indulgence of his son Joseph. Or the tragic story of King David and his headstrong son Absalom, who fomented a conspiracy against his own father. Rabbi Donin refers to a *midrash* (in *Shemot Rabbah* 1:1) on this story which he says emphasizes "the absence of firmness and the unwillingness to discipline children as the basic causes for rebellion against parents."

Citing Abraham's displeasure with his son Ishmael, whom he cast out of his house, another *midrash* warns: "When a person refrains from chastising his son, the son will fall into evil ways, [in this case, idolatry] so that in the end the father will come to hate him." Commenting on this passage in their book *Jewish Parenting: Rabbinic Insights*, Rabbi Judith Z. Abrams and Dr. Steven A. Abrams acknowledge how tedious it can be "to constantly remind children how to behave. . . . However, neglecting this parental duty will lead to unhappy children and parents who can't stand being around them."

For parents who fear their children will think they're "mean" if they set limits, teacher Janice Miles-League has a good answer in a letter to the Baltimore *Sun*, "When Parents Are Afraid of Their Children."[1] "Our children are not our peers: they need our love, tempered with guidance, positive modeling and restrictions." It is natural for children to be unhappy about some parental rules, but setting fair limits shows that you care.

Children are not born with self-control; they need to be taught. Similarly, disciplining does not come naturally to parents; we need to learn how to do it. Positive discipline is an art, and it does get easier as parents master the techniques. The most important messages to convey to your child through positive discipline are that you love him and care about his well-being, and at the same time you expect certain forms of behavior.

When is the right time to start disciplining children? Babies cannot understand or obey rules. They need to learn that they can trust their parents to care for them. However, toddlers (ages one to three) should be taught some basic limits and rules, such as "No, you must not touch the hot stove because you could get hurt." Even if they are not yet talking, they can understand much of what adults say.

As children reach different ages and developmental stages, their needs for discipline change. In addition to the child's age, other criteria parents should consider when determining appropriate discipline include the child's skills and knowledge, safety issues, as well as family rules and values. The most significant factors are the individual child's own unique personality and needs. Children in the same family may need different kinds of discipline. One may be particularly sensitive to yelling but react better to a quiet rebuke, while his brother may be untouched by either approach, responding instead to being removed from the company of others.

To discipline effectively, parents must have realistic expectations

---

[1] *The Sun*, Baltimore, MD, June 4, 1994.

of their children, based on an understanding of their developmental level. What adults *perceive* as misbehavior in a toddler (such as picking up and dropping a vase, which then breaks) may simply be the result of her natural curiosity about how the world works, or an attempt to do something by herself. However, the child still needs to be taught to respect family and social rules and to understand that her actions have consequences.

Testing the limits of parental authority and expressing defiance is normal behavior for preschool and school-age children. Although this behavior may annoy parents, if they understand it, they can use it to teach children how to navigate safely, to behave in the world, while still giving them the freedom they need to grow, explore, and act on their own.

To set realistic expectations of a young child means—as much as possible—to avoid creating situations in which he is likely to misbehave. Taking an overtired three-year-old shopping or on a long outing is inviting trouble. Nor is it realistic to expect a two-year-old to sit quietly through a synagogue service. Anticipating such situations and planning ahead—by bringing along books, quiet toys, and snacks, and by giving the child breaks to stretch, run, and talk—can often eliminate a need to discipline.

When should children be punished? Parents must evaluate what kinds of misbehavior go over their limits and require punishment. Being selective is important, for punishing everything becomes counterproductive. The goal of punishment should always be to get the behavior to stop—without damaging the child's self-esteem. The Talmud says of parents and children, "Let the left hand repel while the right hand draws near." Rabbi Donin comments that "the child should not be permitted to interpret his punishment as a rejection of himself, only a dissatisfaction with the *act* committed." The message to give the child is *not*: "You are a bad *person*," but rather, "What you did broke our rules."

What about physical punishment? It was sanctioned in Biblical times, but even then parents were advised to exercise restraint, and legal limits were later placed on parental power. Judaism's approach to this aspect of child rearing was extremely enlightened, compared to other societies of that time. "When you hit a child, do not hit him with anything but the string of a shoe," said the Talmudic sage, Rav, a rule which the commentator Rashi explained as "a light stroke which can do no harm."

Today, experts in child development agree that corporal punishment has only negative effects. Dr. Morris Wessel, in the medical journal *Pediatrics*,[1] points out that while hitting or spanking may alter behavior for the moment, they are not effective ways to teach a child self-control, discipline, and cooperation. Corporal punishment confuses a child, who can't understand why adults he loves and trusts are attacking him. It teaches him to fear instead of to respect authority. "Physical punishment is humiliating and demeaning, it teaches a child that might makes right, and it can cause permanent physical and psychological harm," Wessel concludes. Finally, corporal punishment comes down to a loss of control by the adult—precisely the opposite of the behavior the parent is trying to teach the child.

The same can be said for other controlling methods of discipline, such as yelling, scolding and lecturing. Many parents resort to these methods out of anger and frustration. If possible, give yourself time and find a way to calm down before disciplining your child. This will also help you treat him fairly and allow your child to deal effectively with his own anger. Your goal is to teach your child how to talk about his feelings without hurting or attacking others.

You are only human, however, so if you do get angry, don't let it linger. Try not to send a child off to school carrying the sting of your anger or feeling terrible about being mad at you. Don't go to sleep angry. Bed time is a good time to talk things over and to find something positive to point out, even in what was a terrible day. Model the ability to apologize after conflict or misunderstanding by acknowledging that you wish you had behaved differently. Even if the child isn't ready to respond yet, she'll still hear the message that you love her.

It is never too late to use positive discipline with children. Situations that seem hopeless are reversible. What may be required is re-

---

[1]Dr. Morris A. Wessel, "The Pediatrician and Corporal Punishment," *Pediatrics* 66 (1980): 639–640, cited in Abrams and Abrams, *Jewish Parenting: Rabbinic Insights*, p. 203.

evaluating and modifying our disciplinary methods to respond to our children's new developmental stages, personality changes, and growing independence.

Positive discipline is about educating and guiding our children, and about reinforcing limits and family values. Elijah ben Solomon Zalman, the Gaon of Vilna, put it this way in a letter to his family two centuries ago: "When you lead your sons and daughters in the good way, [use] discipline that wins the heart's assent."

Learning How to Discipline

1. Think about how you've been defining "discipline." If you've been equating it with "punishment," refocus on the *positive* role of discipline as a way of teaching a child self-control and responsibility for his actions and a way of enhancing his self-esteem.

2. Read or take a course about child development so that you will have realistic expectations and will teach discipline in ways appropriate to your child's age, developmental level, personality, and needs.

3. Practice self-control yourself so that you can avoid methods damaging to a child, such as corporal punishment, shouting, scolding, or insulting.

4. Remember that parents are fallible and have limits, too. If you "lose it," say "I'm sorry." (Some suggestions for handling stress appear in "When Parenting Feels Like an Overwhelming Job" in this volume.)

The Nuts and Bolts of Positive Discipline

"Train up a child in the way he should go, and even when he is old, he will not depart from it." This much-quoted admonition from the book of Proverbs may seem an impossible ideal to parents struggling with their children over discipline issues. The double challenge for parents is to define what is "the way their children should go" and to find how best to guide their children along their way. The concept of positive discipline can help parents do their jobs more effectively.

As presented in the previous chapter, positive discipline is not about controlling children, but about teaching self-control. Positive discipline is a form of building—building self-esteem in children, teaching them to think for themselves, to solve problems, and to communicate. In short, positive discipline is constructing the foundation for a fulfilling adult life.

Dr. Bruno Bettelheim, educator, psychologist and psychiatrist, found that most parents equate "discipline" with "punishment." We have seen that punishment is the least effective way to teach self-control. In *A Good Enough Parent*, Dr. Bettelheim points instead to the dictionary definitions of "discipline," which include "instruction imparted to scholars" and "training that develops self-control, character, or orderly conduct." If a "disciple" is a learner, he asks, "How can one believe that discipline can be *imposed* or *forced* on another person? The best and probably the only way one can turn oneself into a disciplined person is by emulating someone whose example one admires." Dr. Bettelheim says that the most effective teachers are parents who, by their character and conduct, model their own values, thereby inspiring the growth of self-respect in their children.

One of the most important things parents can do, then, is to behave in the ways they want their child to behave. This means, for example, showing how a person with self-control acts—whether it is by speaking politely to a child, picking up after oneself, or observing the law. Criticizing, giving orders, and preaching are far less effective than setting an example.

Here are some specific guidelines for positive discipline. All of these are appropriate for use with young children, and most pertain to older children as well.

- Set limits. With a young child, start with just a few rules. Clearly explain what you expect and your reasons for the rules. These reasons may include safety, health, family values, and teaching the child how to function in the world. Even when they understand the rules, children still need frequent reminders.
- Involve children in making some of the rules. Keep in mind, however, that there will be times when a child's input is not appropriate, and the parent will have to make the rule. Always give children a chance to tell you what they think and feel.
- Explain clearly what the consequences will be if the rules are not followed. Make the severity of the consequence appropriate to the kind of misbehavior. Follow through by applying the consequences. Frequent threats that are not carried out when rules are broken make for ineffective discipline.
- Set routines for meals, bedtime, and chores. Routines help children understand what their parents expect.
- Give children choices, to encourage independent thought and action.
- Recognize the effort and praise the child when he is trying to change his behavior or has improved even a little. Express confidence that he will do better next time.
- Encourage the child to express her feelings. ("I am angry at you because . . .") ("This is scary.")
- Be consistent in your own behavior, and with the disciplinary approaches of your child's other caretakers. Whenever possible,

the adults who are involved need to discuss and decide what rules, boundaries, and values to set for the family, and support each other's efforts in giving the child clear, consistent messages.

- Distinguish the child himself from his negative behavior. Reinforce your love for your child: "I love *you*, even if what you're doing upsets me."

Underlying all of these suggestions is the importance of good communication—between parent and child, and among parents, family members, and others involved in caring for the child.

In spite of a parent's best efforts at discipline, children will sometimes break the rules. When this happens, try to remain calm and do something that is fair, that makes sense, and that will help the child learn not to make the same mistake again, advises Marilyn Gootman of the National Committee for Prevention of Child Abuse. She suggests involving the child in a process of identifying the problem, suggesting and evaluating possible solutions, and choosing a solution to try the next time. This approach teaches the child that "no problem is so great that you cannot solve it, and that you are responsible for your own behavior."

Helpful disciplinary techniques for young children include:

- *diversion*—distracting the child with a toy or substituting another activity
- *"quiet out" time*—removal of the child from a situation to allow him to calm down enough so that the parent can talk about what happened and what rule was broken
- *removal of something important to the child*—such as a favorite game, an activity, or a privilege. Be sure not to take away a young child's blanket or teddy bear; these security objects can help her unwind and feel safe enough to talk over what has happened.
- *behavior modification*—identifying an attainable goal for your child, and rewarding positive behavior, thereby building self-esteem. Stars or stickers on a daily chart acknowledge and reinforce the desired behavior. Once the child reaches the goal, he understands that he is now responsible for achieving it.

These guidelines and techniques help provide structure and teach young children positive discipline. Structure and guidance are equally important in adolescence. Teenagers can handle more privileges and responsibilities than younger children can. But they still need help with setting limits on their freedom and behavior.

While asserting their independence, which is appropriate for this age, adolescents nevertheless need and want attention from their parents. Some excellent advice for parents is offered by two teenagers in *The Jewish Family Book*, by Sharon Strassfeld and Kathy Green. "The best way for parents and children to work out differences constructively is through *communication*, by talking, doing, showing, or any other way to get the point across." Another adds, "I've found that the more I consider my parents' feelings, the more they consider mine."

The problem with parents that teenagers most often cite is "not being listened to." In "Plain Talk about Adolescence," the National Institute of Mental Health suggests the following guidelines for parents to keep communication open:

- Give your undivided attention when your teenager wants to talk to you.
- Try to listen calmly, even when there is a difference of opinion. Don't over-react or start preaching. Concentrate instead on hearing and understanding your child's point of view, and then have a discussion.
- Use a courteous tone of voice, expressing respect.
- Avoid making judgments. This does not mean compromising your values or approving of everything your child does, but try to understand his behavior and feelings, and consider where you can compromise.
- Keep the door open on any subject, no matter how sensitive. Don't hurt the child by belittling, laughing, or humiliating.
- Permit expression of ideas and feelings, even if you disagree. Conversation is a good way for adolescents to try out ideas they are exploring. Give your own views, but respect their right to their views, and their desire for individuality and independence.

- Build your child's self-confidence in his abilities, and express praise and appreciation whenever possible.
- Take an interest in your child's activities and friends, while respecting her privacy.

Although these suggestions are made for teenagers, if parents begin using them with their *young* children, they can build a foundation for healthy communication during adolescence.

What do you do if you feel the situation in your own family—no matter what age your children are—has gotten out of control? Although it will be hard, it is not too late or impossible to teach positive discipline. Start by identifying your priorities. Examine your expectations of your children, and revamp them appropriately. Evaluate how you have been communicating and disciplining. An excellent idea would be to call a family meeting. (See suggestion #4 below.) You can seek help also from the many resources available, such as a teacher, a friend, a rabbi, or a counselor.

Dr. Bruno Bettelheim urges parents to remember our own childhood struggles learning to discipline ourselves, and how it hurt when our parents were not patient or understanding. "The acquisition of self-discipline is a continuous but slow process of many small steps and many backslides," he says. "The parent who is in a hurry *imposes* discipline, whereas *teaching* self-discipline requires time and patience, and trust in the child's doing all on his own the right thing."

These insights give us another way of understanding the advice in Proverbs, cited above: "Train up a child in the way he should go, and even when he is old, he will not depart from it." Literally translated, the verse says, "Educate a youth according to his way." The Hebrew word for "way" is *derech*, a "path" or "road." The "way" can refer to the values parents want to teach their children for a good life. It can also be understood as the individuality of the child: "Educate a youth according to his own nature." Combining these two interpretations is exactly what positive discipline aims to do. By respecting the individuality of each child and teaching in ways appropriate to his or her own nature, parents give the child a solid foundation for life.

Some How To's of Positive Discipline

1. Since the example you set for your child has more impact than lectures, become more conscious of your actions and model the kind of behavior you expect from the child.

2. No matter the age of your children, allow them to express their feelings and opinions. Listen, even if you disagree and come to a different decision.

3. In order to build self-esteem and responsibility, encourage independent thought and action in your child. Offer praise whenever it is appropriate.

4. A family meeting creates an opportunity to get a fresh start on positive discipline. Tell your children honestly how you feel when they behave in certain ways, and let them explain how they feel. Ask them to suggest solutions. In addition to making all family members feel valued, this approach obliges everyone to acknowledge his own responsibilities. Family conferences can be held regularly or as needed. They will help you discover and build on the strengths of your family.

Even "Normal" Families Need Help Now and Then

The dreaded day is here again. Sammy burrows under the covers this Sunday morning as his mother tries to cajole him into getting up. "Do you want to be late for Hebrew school?" she asks. "I'm not going!" shouts Sammy. The battle of wills escalates, until the ten-year-old boy works himself into a full-scale temper tantrum that even his father cannot stop. Eventually, Sammy and his parents are too exhausted to continue. The day lies in ruins.

This scene has been repeating itself regularly for several weeks. Although Sammy controls himself and cooperates during the regular school day, as well as during weekday Hebrew school sessions, he falls apart on Sundays. His parents, Lois and Myron, have tried pleading, threatening, and punishing. Sometimes they take Sammy in the car kicking and screaming; sometimes they give up and let him stay home.

Just as Sammy's parents are at their wits' end, the Hebrew school teacher calls to express concern about the frequent absences. She has also noticed a contrast between his willing participation on weekdays and his withdrawn attitude on the Sundays when he is present. After hearing about the boy's extreme behavior, she asks Myron and Lois if they have considered consulting a professional family therapist.

Sammy's parents are pained by this suggestion. "She must think *we're* crazy," Myron says. "The problem is Sammy." "Maybe there's something really wrong with Sammy," worries Lois. "But what would other people think if they knew he was going to a counselor? It would be a blot on his record for the rest of his schooling." "We should be able to handle our son ourselves," adds Myron. "Besides, even though we both kill ourselves working full-time, on our salaries, we could never afford therapy."

Many parents share this couple's hesitations about family therapy. Along with their own feelings of failure and guilt, parents may be embarrassed to let other people know they have a problem. A common expectation is that the professional is supposed to "fix" the child because the parent cannot do so. If parents better understood the nature and purpose of family therapy, they would be more willing to consider this means of helping themselves and their child when they are under stress.

Family therapy encourages family members to see themselves as parts of a whole, living system. Changing any part of that system affects all the other parts. The purpose of family therapy is to enable each person to make changes that will enhance communication and relationships so that the family can function more efficiently.

What modern family therapy strives to achieve has long been an ideal in Judaism. It is called *shalom bayit*, "the development of a peaceful and harmonious relationship among all members of a household," as defined by Rabbi Hayim Halevy Donin in *To Be a Jew: A Guide to Jewish Observance in Contemporary Life*. "Shalom" comes from the Hebrew root *shalem*, meaning "complete" or "whole." In *Living a Jewish Life: Jewish Traditions, Customs, and Values for Today's Families*, Anita Diamant and Howard Cooper refer to a beautiful metaphor in Jewish tradition which views the home as a *mikdash ma'at*, a little sanctuary. The image connotes both a place of safety and a holy place, where each family member is valued for who he or she is. "The peace of the house is really the health of the house," say Diamant and Cooper, who advocate extending the concept of *shalom bayit* today to support family therapy and other forms of counseling.

How can parents determine the appropriate time to seek family therapy? When a family is facing a situation that seems too complex or overwhelming to handle alone, this is the right time to ask for help. For example, a family member may be experiencing major anxiety or depression, extreme withdrawal, remarkable changes in sleeping and eating patterns, or extreme anger. There may be a feeling that a family member is out of control, or communication may have broken down. Great stress can result from significant family changes, such as birth, death, divorce, remarriage, a move to a new community, a change of school, or other circumstances shaking family stability.

Family therapy helps families in several ways. First, the therapist attempts to address the problems quickly to minimize the harm that a troubling situation is causing the children. Children need to be children, to play, explore, and feel safe. They should not have to carry the responsibilities of adults. The family therapist helps parents separate their issues and needs from those of the children, so that each can be dealt with more effectively. The professional may also suggest special attention to benefit specific family members, with additional therapy for a child, a couple, or an individual.

"Anger in a household is like a worm among sesame seeds," says the Talmud (Sotah 3). Because the seeds are so small, when a worm spoils some, all are affected. Similarly, all parts of the family unit affect each other.

Through sessions with the whole family, the therapist points out patterns of interaction, helps family members define and get what is really important to them, and builds skills of communication and compromise. Parents and children learn to express feelings of anger, pain, and frustration in ways that are less harmful to each other. They also learn to express positive feelings. The goal is to empower each person, to make sure that everybody's needs are satisfied to the fullest extent possible.

After learning that family therapy can often be beneficial without involving a long-term commitment of time and money, Myron and Lois decided to try it. They chose a therapist they felt comfortable with, who helped them explain to Sammy that they all wanted to work together to resolve what was a family problem. During their early sessions, Myron and Lois realized that Sammy's behavior was a way of asking for attention he needed, but was not getting because of his parents' very demanding work schedules. Sammy acted up on

Sunday mornings, the time when both his parents were home. While he actually liked his Hebrew school teacher, Sammy made going to class the focus of his anger because it happened to conflict with his desire for time with his parents.

During therapy, Lois and Myron explained to Sammy that they couldn't give up their jobs and that Hebrew school was still a priority. However, they could set aside specific times to be with their child individually, as well as planning more family activities. They decided to set aside part of each Shabbat for special family togetherness. Indeed, say Diamant and Cooper in *Living a Jewish Life*, "Shabbat has always been and continues to be the basic building block of family peace. Creating a restful island of time—turning off the television and turning to one another—can actually prevent injury from the wear and tear of the week. It can heal wounds that were not even apparent."

As therapy helped Sammy learn how to ask for attention in ways that his parents could hear, his parents worked on giving him their undivided attention at more appropriate times. Lois and Myron also realized that they needed to spend more time with each other. By strengthening their marital relationship, they could also better meet Sammy's needs for a secure, loving home. Implementing these changes took work and cooperation. The Sunday morning battles ceased. After a few months of therapy, the family was functioning in a much healthier way and no longer felt the need for professional assistance.

With more information, parents may overcome the hesitation to embark on therapy when overwhelmed by a problem. It can be helpful for parents to remember that they control the process; they hire the therapist and have a right to seek a match that feels comfortable. When a family undertakes therapy on its own, this is a private affair. The therapist, parents and children (depending on their ages and levels of understanding) decide what information, if any, will be given to whom. The therapist can serve as an advocate for the child, for example, in the school. When an outside source, such as the school, police, court system, or Department of Social Services, recommends therapy, the family's confidentiality is still a priority, and they are involved in decisions about releasing information if necessary. The duration of therapy can vary, depending on the nature of the problem, and the cost can be affordable. Some expenses may be covered by health plans.

At some point, every family needs help and support. Beginning therapy may seem harder than living with problems, because it requires awareness of one's own and other family members' needs and feelings, as well as changes in behavior. By involving the whole family, this kind of therapy helps family members get in touch with their individual strengths and define their needs, resulting in enhanced communication. The rewards of the effort are what parents wish for themselves and their children: strengthened family life and healthier relationships—in a nutshell, *shalom bayit.*

It's OK for Parents to Ask for Help

1. Family therapy offers parents and children a constructive way out of the isolation and frustration they feel when they are under stress.

2. In selecting a family therapist, parents should look for a professional who has at least a master's degree in a mental health field such as social work, psychology, or counseling, with additional training and interest in family therapy.

3. "At its best, sharing family life in Jewish ways is a technique for making peace," say Anita Diamant and Howard Cooper in *Living a Jewish Life.* We can help make our homes into "little sanctuaries" of peace, beauty, and joy by observing *mitzvot* (commandments) such as Shabbat and hospitality, and by decorating our homes with Jewish art and ritual objects that we use.

The Power of Laughter

Half an hour before the children's bedtime, the household is in an uproar—T.V. blaring, dog barking, brother and sister in the midst of a shouting argument. Mom's efforts to restore order are falling on deaf ears. Suddenly, Dad comes up from his basement workshop. He grabs the kids and starts roughhousing with them. As the dog joins in, the noise escalates. Surveying the chaos, Mom suddenly points to Dad and announces, "You—you go on *time out*." A surprised pause—and everyone begins to laugh.

Minor crises happen every day in families. To weather these moments, and to get perspective on our job as parents, we need a healthy dose of humor. In *Meditations for Parents Who Do Too Much*, Jonathon and Wendy Lazear point out the need "to get some distance on our lives. We need to realize those things that we can change for the better and those things we are powerless to change. Laughing may not be the remedy for everything, but it certainly lightens our load."[1]

Long ago, our ancestors Abraham and Sarah had a good laugh when they were promised that they would become parents at ages 90 and 100, after Sarah had suffered years of barrenness. Sure enough, along came a son, whose name, by divine command, was Isaac, which in Hebrew means *laughter*. Although the Bible does not relate playful scenes between Isaac and his parents—on the con-

---

[1]Jonathan and Wendy Lazear, *Meditations for Parents Who Do Too Much*, New York: Fireside/Parkside, Simon and Schuster, Inc., 1993, entry for May 22.

trary, his near-sacrifice was surely traumatic—perhaps Isaac's name carries a message for parents about the importance of humor in family life.

One way to find the humor in parenting is to remember what it was like for us when we were children. "Benny," said his father, "your hands are filthy. Have you ever seen my hands like that?" "No, dad," answers Benny, "but maybe your father did."[1] We were all young once; we misbehaved, got into trouble, and made mistakes. We lacked the breadth of experience of adults, their common sense and logic.

It is important to let our children see us as vulnerable and fallible. "Did I ever tell you about the time I broke a window with my football? Or the time I cut my little sister's hair? Boy, did I get into big trouble!" And we can laugh at the mistakes we make as adults: "Can you believe I forgot to pack my bathing suit for vacation?" "When I got down to the cellar, I forgot what I was going there for." The key to Jewish humor, says David C. Gross in *Laughing through the Years*, is the ability to laugh at oneself. When we can do this with our children, we let them know it is O.K. to make mistakes, and that adults are not perfect.

Judaism recognizes the enjoyment young children get when they see adults act silly and undignified. In fact, we have two holidays when we are *commanded* to behave in just that way. On Purim, adults and kids alike wear costumes and make noise in synagogue where children are usually hushed. On Simchat Torah, we dance, sing, and make merry. It is customary on both holidays to perform parodies and set prayers to unexpected melodies. Letting out the child in ourselves at these times is healthy and enriches family life.

In daily life, humor can be a very useful tool for defusing family tensions. The woman who banished her husband to "time out" used the element of surprise effectively. Another mother ended nightly battles with her five-year-old over cleaning his teeth by making funny faces and encouraging him to imitate them while brushing.

A good place for humor is where parents and children today

[1]Rufus Learsi, *Filled with Laughter: A Fiesta of Jewish Folk Humor*, New York: Thomas Yoseloff, 1961.

spend a lot of time—in the car. When sibling conflicts break out, try singing loudly. Telling jokes and reciting silly rhymes are effective ways to decrease boredom or restlessness with younger children.

Children often do things that evoke parents' disapproval. Instead of confrontation and overt criticism, we can sometimes stop the behavior with humor. For example, try telling a young child who is using bathroom language inappropriately to repeat the word 100 times. After a while, it becomes ludicrous, and the silliness extinguishes the behavior. Have two fighting siblings impose "time out" on each other, each relegated to a chair and forbidden to get up until the other gives permission. This distracts them by becoming a game, and it also gets the parent out of the middle.

With pre-teens and teens, self-directed humor works better. The first time your teenager comes home past curfew, instead of the heavy-handed approach, try: "I remember I did that once, and my parents were so worried that they called the police. The cops drove up and saw me and my boyfriend sitting in the car down the street from our house. Boy, was I embarrassed. After that I came home on time."

Although there are times to laugh, parents need to decide when to exert their authority. Trying to be the child's best friend is not in his or her best interest. It is important to maintain some boundaries.

Like adults, children also use humor. Kids enjoy attention and making adults laugh. Little ones will clown, and children of all ages may themselves use humor to reduce family friction. Understanding a child's sense of humor can be very helpful to parents. What children find funny depends on their temperaments, ages, and developmental levels. Up to age 4, children's humor is largely visual; for example, they make faces. From 4 to 6, they laugh at silly words, rhymes, knock-knock jokes, and slightly scary games like hiding and jumping out. From age 7, when they start reading, children's humor becomes more verbal, and by age 9 they can appreciate puns. Pre-teenagers like practical jokes and trying on different roles, as part of the process of self-discovery. The influence of peers is paramount for teens, whose humor centers on the foibles of their friends.

To find out what tickles your child, listen to her laughter, and investigate what triggers it—which jokes, books, cartoons, TV shows. Sometimes you can share the humor. But even when you don't find it funny, you can pick up clues that can be used to get her to laugh at a tense moment in the future.

When what children find funny does not amuse adults for more serious reasons, parents need to set boundaries. Children will test parents by using vulgar language or telling jokes focusing on bodily functions and noises. Preteen girls do a lot of whispering, giggling, and gossiping. Parents need to point out that this behavior is not acceptable when it is a breach of good manners or when it hurts someone's feelings. However, the experience of sharing humor with peers is one that parents should not entirely deny their children. It is alright to tell certain kinds of jokes in certain contexts, such as slumber parties or camping trips. Children need permission to unwind with their friends, as long as it is not harmful behavior. Remember that we do this with our peers, too.

Humor sometimes results from children's naïveté. As they try to make sense of the world, they may take language literally, making observations or asking questions that adults find amusing. Joey asked his father, "There's something in the Bible I can't figure out. It says the Children of Israel crossed the Red Sea, and the Children of Israel beat up the Philistines; they built the Temple, and they fought the Romans. The Children of Israel were always doing something important. What I want to know is what were the grown-ups doing all that time?"[1]

When children come up with these gems, an affectionate smile is fine, but avoid mocking them or otherwise hurting their feelings. Try to understand their reasoning. Humor should never be used at the child's expense. As the Yiddish proverb says, "A wounded spirit is hard to heal."

"Parenting is too important to be taken seriously," says Dr. Ray Guarendi of the Children's Hospital Medical Center in Akron, Ohio.[2] If we try too hard, striving to be perfect parents, this diminishes our effectiveness. If we let them, our children will teach us to

---

[1] Henry Spalding, *A Treasure Trove of American Jewish Humor*, p. 61.

[2] Dr. Ray Guarendi, "The Parenting Facts of Life," *McCall's*, April 1991, pp. 91–94.

laugh. Childhood passes so quickly; humor can help us enjoy it even more.

Tips to Tickle Family Funny Bones

1. Pause before responding to a tense situation with your children, and look for any humor that can avert an explosion.

2. Lighten the mood by telling a joke, making a comparison your child can relate to, or telling about humorous incidents from your childhood.

3. Bring up private family jokes like "Remember that time Grandma left the sugar out of the Hanukkah cookies?" to defuse frictions.

4. Use humor as a respite from an overscheduled lifestyle. Have a family fun day when you do silly things at home like watch old movies, dress up, or play a game at which no one is very skilled.

Sensitive Issues

Money Matters

Some homespun wisdom about money from a collection of Yiddish proverbs teaches that "It's not money that makes everything good; it's that no money makes everything bad." "It is easier to make money than to keep it." "A full purse is not so good as an empty one is bad."

Like it or not, we cannot be indifferent to and unaffected by money. "Money is often a source of underlying tension, overt hostility, and chronic conflict" in families, asserts Olivia Mellon, a psychotherapist who specializes in the psychology of money and money conflict resolution. "For most of us, money is *never* just money," says Mellon. "It represents some combination of love, power, security, dependency, freedom, control, and self-worth."

The emotions and significance we attach to money stem from childhood. Whether deliberately or unwittingly, our families communicated certain messages about money to us: "money corrupts," "money must be saved for a rainy day," or "money should be spent because you can't take it with you." As adults, we may find ourselves repeating these patterns or, conversely, reacting against them. In turn, we influence our children's attitudes. By observing how we handle money, children reach conclusions about what is important in their family: appearance, possessions, education, philanthropy, or any other value.

In an article called "Reflections on the Family, Tzedakah and Transmitting Jewish Values," psychologist and UJA/Federation leader David Arnow observes that "families tend to relate to issues involving money with discomfort and outright avoidance. . . . As a result, many parents miss the opportunity of making the home a place where children can learn from their example."

Money is a wonderful vehicle for parents to teach their children values and prepare them for adult life. In learning how to manage money, children gain experience in planning, making choices, and taking responsibility. This is a continuous process which is most effective when parents first clarify their own attitudes towards money and act consistently.

Preschool is a good time to start teaching children financial responsibility. Young children think in concrete terms. If they are given the freedom to spend a specified amount of money as they see fit, they will learn that when it's gone, it's gone. But parents must be willing to let their kids make some mistakes, and not bail them out. The risks can be controlled by directing the money for a particular purpose. For example, on an outing to the annual Jewish Festival, Jane and Lenny give each of their twins $5.00 with the message, "This is it for the day." Now the boys have the freedom to make individual choices about how to spend the money. These early lessons in reality prepare children for planning and budgeting later. "You are empowering them to run parts of their lives," says Neale Godfrey, author of *Money Doesn't Grow on Trees: A Parent's Guide to Raising Financially Responsible Children.*

Most parents set about teaching children the value of money in one of two ways: by giving them money as needed or as a regular allowance, or by having them work to earn the money. One option is to mix these models, deciding at what age each is appropriate and most conducive to learning.

A regular allowance is an excellent way to teach money management. Some parents link the allowance to household chores, thus teaching their children that money comes from work. Others believe children should be expected to fulfill household responsibilities as members of the family, with no pay. The allowance is kept separate from those jobs. Still others give an allowance but provide extra money for certain household responsibilities. There are pros and cons to each of these approaches, and each communicates a family's values. For example, paying Susan to do her chores can be an incentive, but does she then have the right to refuse a job and forego the money? One way to resolve this is to give Susan her allowance when all her chores are done.

In deciding on the amount and timing of an allowance, first consider your family's income and standard of living. Then, factor in your child's age, needs, and ability to budget. With a young child, start with small amounts for specific events (a movie or family outing) when he is able to carry money in his pocket without losing it. For the schoolage child who begins to venture out into environments without adults, there are different opportunities to spend money, such as school lunches, snacks, or video games. A teenager wants to buy clothes and music, gas for the car, and entertainment on dates. "Lengthening the time between allowances is a way of shifting more responsibility onto older kids and teaching budgeting," says Lynn Asinof in a *Wall Street Journal* article on "Kids and Money".[1] Keep in mind that the amount given must realistically reflect the current cost of living.

Another source of income is money earned by working outside the home. Middle schoolers cut lawns, shovel snow, or babysit; high school students may have steady jobs. While most parents allow young children to keep their earnings, later on parents can look at their philosophy and financial circumstances with their teenagers, deciding whether some of the young adults' earnings will be contributed back to the family "pot" or to future educational expenses.

Children also receive gifts of money—for birthdays, Hanukkah, Bar Mitzvah and graduation. A painful scene in *The Loman Family Picnic*, by Donald Margulies, brings into stark relief the question: who controls the money given to children? In this play about a hardworking father and his family searching for the American dream in 1960s Brooklyn, young Stewie is shocked on the night after his Bar Mitzvah when his father demands the cash to help offset the expense of the extravagant party they have just thrown.

---

[1]Lynn Asinof, "Kids and Money: Lessons on Dollars and Sense." *The Wall Street Journal*, Nov. 19, 1993.

It is vital for parents to be clear about what power a child has over money, whether it comes to him through gifts, allowance, or earnings. Gifts, by definition, should have fewer strings attached, and children deserve to spend some of the money they have earned. However, each parent needs to set, and discuss with the child, the limits of parental approval, and these decisions should be consistent with the family's values. For example, if Linda gets to keep a portion of her Bat Mitzvah money, she may have to spend it on something other than a T.V. or a private telephone for her room if these conflict with family guidelines. When a child follows the guidelines, parents need to be prepared to respect the child's choice, even if it may not reflect their own tastes or priorities.

One essential lesson to be learned is how to balance spending and saving. Jeffrey Picker, a C.P.A. with Arthur Andersen and Company, says that requiring a child to save *all* his money doesn't teach him its value. "Money is a commodity to be used to acquire things; we must teach the responsibility of managing money." Neale Godfrey suggests having children divide their allowance into three parts: the first can be spent right away; the second is short-term savings for something special; and the third is long-term savings. There are all kinds of savings plans; "the main thing is to create a system that both you and your kids like so that you will stick with it," says Godfrey. And parents need to discuss what the savings are *for*: education, emergencies, vacations, retirement.

David Arnow points out that parents often overestimate the level of their children's understanding of many aspects of their adult world, including their financial commitments. Indeed, for a variety of reasons, some parents choose to tell their children nothing about their incomes or budget, while others share more. Children need to know that parents' earnings are private family information, and that parents have the right to maintain discretion and set boundaries. Parents should consider why the child is asking: is it simple curiosity, or is the child feeling worried and insecure because he has heard the parents talking about not having enough money? One approach is to give partial information, such as, "This week we have $25 in our family entertainment fund," and to emphasize the general principle that the amount spent must be based on the amount earned.

A family budget and a family standard of spending will teach responsibility and consistency. Parents need to involve their children in discussions about money, particularly when decisions affect them. When a family is under financial stress, says C.P.A. Jeffrey Picker, children can sense there is a problem, and parents should be honest. If they can no longer maintain the same lifestyle, they should not try to live beyond their means for the children's sake. Avoid putting guilt on children by such remarks as, "We can't go on a vacation because we are paying for private school" . . . or for special tutoring for a sibling with a disability, or any other expenses.

Sharon Strassfeld and Kathy Green summarize lessons about the value of money in *The Jewish Family Book.* "We want to teach our children that money represents effort, and that it should be budgeted wisely. We want them to learn the value of things. We don't want them to value money too much and worship it. But we don't want them to value it so much that they will find it difficult to spend appropriately or to give money away to *tzedakah.*"

In fact, says Rabbi Daniel Lehmann, teaching children about the value of *tzedakah* may be as important as teaching them about financial management. Parents can help their children decide what charitable contributions they should make and how much of their money they should give to others in need. Judaism has generally considered 10% (a tithe) to be the average amount that should be donated to tzedakah, while 20% is thought to be very generous. A beautiful custom increasingly practiced is for a Bar or Bat Mitzvah to donate a portion of the money received as gifts to a charity that is meaningful to the child. Parents can model this sharing by following the suggestion of MAZON: A Jewish Response to Hunger to donate 3% of the cost of their *simcha,* or by giving to any other worthy cause.

Tzedakah can be a family endeavor which will bring a distinctively Jewish element to the family's financial matters while teaching the entire family about one of Judaism's most cherished values.

Each family defines its own values and finds its own way of teaching children financial responsibility and management. Even within the same family, the individual personalities and amount of independence of each child will help determine what is the most effective approach for parents to take with that child. The two essential ingredients in this process are working out a family plan or system, and communicating with all family members.

Pecuniary Pointers for Parents

1. Daily life offers many opportunities for informal lessons about money management that are fun for children, such as keeping track of tolls and restaurant expenses when travelling, or using coupons and making change in the grocery store. Set up a savings account for your child and watch the interest accrue.

2. Teach teenagers about more complicated financial realities such as taxes on their earnings, the responsible use of credit cards, and long-term investments.

3. Make your own family *tzedakah* box with your children, or choose a beautiful one together at a Judaica store or synagogue gift shop. Make *tzedakah* a habit by establishing a pattern, such as giving each week before Shabbat and before Rosh Hashanah, Purim, Passover, and other holidays. Share with your children the decision-making process of determining where your *tzedakah* is given. Discuss the child's particular concerns or interests and see if a charitable organization can be found that addresses those issues. Get involved as a family in "hands-on" *tzedakah* projects such as working in a soup kitchen.

4. Be aware that today's economic realities differ from those of our childhood. We may need to develop different approaches to financial management than our parents used.

Talking with Your Child about Sexuality

Why do many parents find it difficult to discuss sexuality with their children? "Although I feel I have good communication with my kids, I admit I've avoided bringing up this subject," says Marty, the father of three children ranging in age from 5 to 14. Janice, who has two children in elementary school, says, "When my kids ask about sexual matters, I try to answer helpfully, but sometimes it just feels awkward."

A guide by Planned Parenthood titled *How to Talk with Your Child about Sexuality* notes that parents are uncomfortable for a variety of reasons: Their own parents did not discuss sex or treated it as something shameful; they fear revealing their ignorance of some information; or they have difficulty acknowledging their children's or their own sexuality. In addition, some parents feel ambivalent about their own values; others worry that giving their children information may be construed as sanctioning sexual activity.

Treating sexuality as a taboo subject creates a barrier between parent and child. Through their parents' silence, their non-verbal as well as verbal reactions, children soon perceive that adults consider sexuality an explosive topic. To get over this hurdle of reticence, we need to relate sexuality to other kinds of experiences, rather than view it as an isolated part of our lives, says Rabbi Daniel Lehmann, who, as past Principal of the Upper School at Beth Tfiloh Community School, discussed sexuality, among other topics, in sessions with students and parents.

To embark on such a discussion, we first need a clear and comprehensive definition of sexuality. Our culture generally uses a limited definition, equating "sex" with "the facts of life"—that is, reproduction, and specifically the act of sexual intercourse, according to Deborah M. Roffman, who teaches human sexuality education at several secular, day, and religious schools in the Baltimore area, and who consults nationally on this topic. But human sexuality is "perhaps the most fundamental component of our total identity," maintains Roffman. "Sexuality encompasses all of the ways we think, feel, behave, and relate to others because we are either male or female. Sexuality includes both our 'genitality' (our genital behavior) and our 'genderality.'"

Children learn about their sexuality from many sources, including self-exploration, parents and other family members, peers, sexual partners, schools, other institutions (clubs, scouts, religious institutions), books, mass media, and health professionals, says Richard Cross, M.D., in an article called "Helping Adolescents Learn about Sexuality."[1] Dr. Cross says adults must help children sort out the often confusing sources of information on sexuality that daily compete for their attention.

By involving their children in an ongoing dialogue about human sexuality, parents can help them develop personal attitudes and values that will guide them throughout life. In talking with children of any age, three questions parents should consider are: What does my child already know? What does he want to know? At what level of understanding can he receive the information?

Mental health professionals today encourage beginning a child's sexual education early. Here are some pointers for parents of young children.

- Explain the anatomical differences between boys and girls early. (Most three-year-olds can begin to understand this information.)
- Use plain language and a matter-of-fact manner. Call body parts by their proper names.

---

[1]Richard J. Gross, M.D., "Helping Adolescents Learn About Sexuality," *SIECUS Report*, April/May 1991.

- Read relevant books with your children, and leave books in accessible locations around the house for your children to pick up on their own.
- If beginning is hard, it's perfectly O.K. to say, "You know, my parents didn't talk to me about sex, and I wish they had. I'm finding this a little difficult, but I think it's important." Such candor will usually break the ice and bring you closer to your child, making conversation easier.

To prepare for dialogue with your child, it is important first to engage in some self-examination and discussion with your spouse. Single and divorced parents can also undertake this process of reflection. As your child approaches puberty, look at your own feelings about gender, sexuality, and health. What issues are likely to come up in discussions with your child, and how do you feel about them? Some issues to consider are contraception, pregnancy, rape, sexually transmitted diseases, homosexuality, and a range of ways to express deep feelings for and intimacy with another person. What are the social, personal, and health consequences of sexual behavior before marriage, and what are the reasons for and consequences of reserving sexual intercourse for marriage?

Go through some possible scenarios, discussing how you would handle them. For example, would you allow your teenager to attend a coed sleepover party? How do you feel about limits on your child's privacy? What would you do if your teen invited a friend into his or her room and locked the door? Your own views may still be evolving, especially as you see how your child handles these issues, but at least you will be ready to communicate accurate information, some guidelines and values.

What happens when two parents can't discuss or don't agree? Try to avoid emotional arguments in front of the children by working out differences between you first. If the disagreements can't be resolved, it is better to be open, and present both views to the child. Counseling with a trusted adult, such as a social worker, rabbi, teacher, physician, or family friend, can help adolescents struggling to make up their own minds about what sexual behavior and values are right for them, and can benefit parents as well.

One of the biggest challenges for parents is to try to understand how their children are experiencing issues of sexuality in *today's* world. The messages one generation gives the next are rooted in the social, religious, medical, and legal issues of their time. For example, views about contraception and abortion, as well as the availability of these options, have changed since the time when parents of today's teens were adolescents. The menace of AIDS, which took us by surprise, motivated us to deal proactively with our children's sexual health, says Deborah Roffman. Since AIDS, she sees an increase in communication between parents and kids partly because, with the media using more direct, explicit language every day, our culture has given permission for freer conversations about sex in families, schools, and other venues.

In spite of changes over time, one tradition that has conducted open discussion about sexuality for millennia is Judaism, which offers a framework that is extraordinary in what it can teach us today. "Judaism recognizes the centrality of sexuality and its tremendous allure in human life," says Rabbi Daniel Lehmann. Sexuality is freely and explicitly discussed in Biblical and rabbinic literature. For example, the Song of Songs, which is read publicly in synagogues on Passover, celebrates the naturalness, beauty, and joy of human sexuality as a metaphor for our relationship with God. The Talmud is aware of our strong sexual urge, but teaches that, to be meaningful, sexuality must be an expression of trust and intimacy, recognizing and respecting the "personhood" of another in a relationship. A medieval manual on marital sex, *Iggeret Hakodesh* (The Holy Letter), portrays the sexual experience as potentially a holy act.[1]

Rabbi Lehmann encourages teenagers, through discussion, to explore the tension between what draws us to sexuality and what can make it holy. What is the best context for expressing this form of communication? Using analogies with other experiences, Rabbi Lehmann talks about powerful things, like language, which lose strength through overuse and misuse. "Holiness means safeguarding something powerful so that its power can be used and expressed appropriately," he says, illustrating this concept with the examples

[1] *The Holy Letter (Iggeret Hakodesh)*, translated by Seymour J. Cohen. New York: KTAV Publishing House, 1976.

of Shabbat and the custom of keeping the Torah in an ark. He finds that teenagers have "an innate sense that something as powerful as sex should not be used in a common way. What could be more powerful than the fact that the sexual act can produce another human being, a link to the future?"

In *Jewish Parenting: Rabbinic Insights*, Rabbi Judith Z. Abrams and Dr. Steven A. Abrams point out that our rabbis centuries ago encouraged marriage at a young age, so that adolescent sexual drives would be appropriately channelled. Strict guidelines were set down to ensure separation of young men and women so as to avoid temptations—guidelines which are still part of the Orthodox tradition.

Marriage in our society generally comes later. Rabbi Lehmann is among those who believe that "because marriage is the only context in which total trust and permanence of relationship can be established, sexuality best retains its sacred and healthy qualities within marriage." The role of adults, he says, is to help adolescents understand the power of sexuality and make reasoned choices about how this power should be used. This entails adults' articulating and modelling their own values about relationships and intimacy.

While recognizing the "plurality of opinion in our culture about acceptable and unacceptable non-marital sexual behavior," Deborah Roffman maintains that "all adults can agree that we want to raise our children to become sexually healthy and happy people." With this positive focus, we avoid giving our kids mixed messages and becoming mired in the either-or arguments between those preaching abstinence and those advocating "safe sex" with contraception. Roffman stresses that teaching the components of human sexuality—the facts of life, gender and relationships—and developing the skills of critical thinking, reasoning, decision-making, and communicating, is an ongoing process. Young people tend to overestimate what they know, and they can't always distinguish accurate from inaccurate information. As they mature, they still need information about the same topics, but in more sophisticated ways. Parents need not worry that "knowing leads to doing"; instead, it leads to more responsible behavior.

The developmental task of teenagers is to become independent young adults. As parents, we have the right and responsibility to tell our children, at any age, what is important to us and why. In a world in which children have more freedom than we did at their age, we hope our adolescents will give careful consideration to our views before acting. "We need to convey our respect for [our children's] ability to make responsible decisions for themselves even as we seek to give them the Jewish values through which their personal freedom will find its proper fulfillment," write Dr. Estelle Borowitz, a psychoanalyst, and Rabbi Eugene B. Borowitz, professor of education and Jewish religious thought, in *The Jewish Family Book*, by Sharon Strassfeld and Kathy Green.

It is especially important to keep communication open with adolescents by discussing aspects of sexuality with them *beforehand*, because emotions usually will be the driving force at the time they act. Parents need to discuss their worries and concerns with their children about sexual health issues such as pregnancy and disease prevention, and they also need to share their attitudes and values regarding the appropriateness of sexual behavior itself. It is helpful to keep these levels of the conversation separate to avoid giving unclear messages. For example, when a parent tells a teenager, "I don't want you to get a disease," does she really mean, "I don't want you to have sex"? Other issues often included in discussions of sex, but that should be examined individually, include drug and alcohol use, driving, body image, and what attracts a person to others.

Here is some advice for parents of teenagers. Some of the suggestions come from young adults just beyond their teen years.

- Be aware of the extent of peer pressure, even in the early teen years, to experiment sexually before marriage.
- Teenagers often view the need to take practical precautions as interfering with their romantic image of love.
- Advise adolescents to prepare themselves by thinking and talking about what they would do in various situations *before* these arise. For example, before going to a party or out on a date, they need to know their capacity to remain in control and decide what limits they will set on their own behavior.

- Consider whether you are willing to share with your child some of your own teenage experiences and what you learned from them. Remember, however, that you also have a right to privacy.

It is never too late to discuss human sexuality with your child. As important as discussion is, however, parents still have a significant impact through the behavior they model for their children. As Deborah Roffman says, parents contribute in countless ways to their children's healthy sexual development, by physical expressions of their love, and by "nurturing their self-esteem, teaching them responsibility to self and others, and allowing themselves to be demonstrably human and vulnerable. All of these experiences . . . become the cornerstone of the adult capacity for intimacy."

Suggestions for Teaching About Sexuality

1. Create an open atmosphere that encourages children to ask questions. If your communication about other subjects has been built on trust, your child will feel comfortable asking about sexuality as well.

2. Use events touching the child's own life (such as the pregnancy of a friend or relative) to start conversations.

3. Use school assignments (in biology, literature, physical education), news stories, and movies and television shows that your child watches as openers for family discussion of sexuality issues.

4. You don't have to deal with all of this alone. Many resources are available to parents, including books, schools, community professionals, and parent workshops and support groups.

Escaping from the Body Trap

One day, Mrs. C. received a phone call that her daughter Jennifer had been taken to the hospital after passing out at school. The sixteen-year-old had been experiencing dizziness, fatigue, and loss of concentration for some time—symptoms she had kept to herself. At 5 feet 6 inches, Jen now weighed 80 pounds. After medical examination, Jennifer was diagnosed as suffering from *anorexia nervosa,* an eating disorder.

"How did this happen to our daughter?" Jen's parents wondered. It was a process evolving over several years. Jen had been a compliant child, and excelled as a student. However, she could not seem to please her family enough. In addition, as a preteen, Jen felt fat and unattractive. Before her Bat Mitzvah, she put herself on a strict diet because she dreaded not being thin enough when appearing before all those people. For the next few years, she had episodes of dieting and bingeing. As she later put it, she felt "trapped in an unacceptable body."

After they became aware of Jen's eating disorder, her parents felt ashamed and guilty. They feared being judged as failures by professionals. Mr. and Mrs. C. soon learned that Jen's only hope of recovery was treatment, and began a process of education about her illness.

Eating disorders are serious emotional problems that can have life-threatening physical consequences, as explained in "Eating Disorders: Questions and Answers," a publication of Sheppard Pratt Hospital. An eating disorder is characterized by an obsession with food, weight and body image, resulting in behaviors focused on eating, getting rid of, or avoiding food. Four main types of eating disorders are *anorexia nervosa*, characterized by an intense fear of gaining weight, leading to self-starvation, and excessive weight loss; *bulimia nervosa*, a secretive cycle of binge eating (eating large amounts of food) and purging to get rid of the food (by vomiting, laxatives, diuretics, or excessive exercise); *compulsive overeating*, which is uncontrollable eating followed by dieting and exercise; and *binge eating*, which is similar to bulimia without the purging. Many people struggle with two or more of these disorders in a cyclical pattern.

Ninety to ninety-five percent of the time, eating disorders occur in women, according to Kathryn J. Zerbe, M.D. in *The Body Betrayed*. David Roth, Ph.D., Director of Sheppard Pratt's Eating Disorders Programs, says that 1–2% of adolescent and young adult women are anorexic, and 4–7% are bulimic. There are more male compulsive overeaters than male anorexics and bulimics. Eating disorders usually become evident in the teenage years, but anorexia can also occur in women in their forties and fifties. An eating disorder can become a lifelong illness if not treated, and at worst, leads to death, says Mary Sachs, community health nurse at JFS.

Moses Maimonides, the great medieval Jewish philosopher and physician, said, "The excessive desire for eating [and] drinking . . . brings diseases and afflictions upon body and soul alike."[1] In the communal confession we recite on Yom Kippur, we ask forgiveness "for the sin of eating and drinking," suggesting that overindulgence is common. But how can we tell when a person has an eating disorder and is no longer within the "normal" range of eating behavior? This is particularly challenging for parents of adolescent girls.

Most girls and women in our culture are concerned about their weight and figure. Teenage girls discuss eating, share diet tips, and size each other up to see who is thinnest. This does not mean they all have eating disorders. Wishing to look thinner in a bathing suit, or comforting ourselves with food after a rough day are feelings common to most women, says Dr. Zerbe.

---

[1] Maimonides, *The Guide of the Perplexed*, III, 12, quoted in Jacob S. Minken, *The Teachings of Maimonides*, Northvale, NJ: Jason Aronson Inc., 1987, p. 221.

Eating behavior becomes unhealthy when a person who lacks other ways to deal with feelings and stressful situations uses food as a way of coping and escaping. One recovered anorexic describes her journey in the newsletter of the Maryland Association for Anorexia Nervosa and Bulimia (MAANA): "It wasn't the food—throwing it away or giving it to the dog—it was how I dealt with stress in my life. Looking at my body, observing other women, and restricting what I ate was my way of avoiding the real struggles."

Eating disorders are the symptoms, but the central issue is self-esteem, says Mary Sachs. The anorexic, as portrayed in *Surviving an Eating Disorder*, by Siegel, Drisman, and others, is typically a perfectionist, critical of herself, and accustomed to accommodating to others. She may begin dieting like anyone else, but, in losing weight, she finds she now has *control* in a life in which she previously did not feel effective or strong. Dieting, binge eating, and purging are ways to declare her independence. Once she feels this power, the young woman is loathe to relinquish it. She shrouds her problem in secrecy and denial. Thus, she is caught in a trap, her eating behavior further undermining her health and self-esteem.

Eating disorders are complicated problems with no single explanation. Some people are genetically or biologically predisposed. According to the Sheppard Pratt Eating Disorders Programs staff, the causes are thought to be a combination of longstanding emotional, psychological, and social conditions. Family and personal relationships may play significant roles. A chaotic home life, the unavailability of parents to their children, excessive control and expectations, abusive relationships, and lack of support for expressing feelings all have been associated with eating disorders.

Our culture's obsession with image and weight is also partially to blame. Attesting to the search for thinness and beauty is the proliferation of diet clinics, weight reduction vacations, diet pills, and exercise programs. Movies, television, magazines, and billboards bombard us with images of "the beautiful body." Barbie dolls are as popular as ever. While these messages have primarily targeted women, men are increasingly conscious of diet and body image. Eating disorders are especially common in some professions which emphasize weight, such as dance, fashion modeling, and sports.

The complex causes and forms of eating disorders can seem overwhelming to parents, but there are things parents can do to prevent their child from developing an eating disorder. Most important is to create an environment in which your child feels free to express *any* feelings without being criticized or belittled. A child who feels that home is a safe and supportive place won't need to resort to eating as an escape from feelings and powerlessness.

Examine your own attitudes toward and behavior with food, and ask what messages you are giving your child. Are you constantly dieting or working out? Do you criticize yourself or others for being "too fat"? Is food used in your home to cheer up someone who is sad? Is compliant behavior rewarded with dessert or candy? Do you label certain foods "good" or "bad," or yourself "good" or "bad" for eating them? Eating Disorders Awareness and Prevention (EDAP), a group of mental health professionals that disseminates educational materials to increase awareness and prevention of eating disorders, points out that children learn messages about body image and food at very young ages. Many six and seven-year-olds are already dissatisfied with their body size, and most girls start dieting before reaching their teens. EDAP urges parents to teach their children: "Don't weigh your self-esteem—It's what's inside that counts."

What should you do if you are worried that a child close to you has an eating disorder? Although much of the behavior is secret, there are warning signs. Look for mood changes or swings; striking changes in weight (loss or gain); changes in eating habits; a preoccupation with weight and body image; use of laxatives or diet pills; vomiting; and excessive exercising. It may seem difficult to distinguish what are normal adolescent changes, but *you know your child best*. Listen to your intuitions, and take the initiative by calling an eating disorders clinic or hotline. The gravity of an eating disorder should not be minimized or denied; early detection and action can be very effective.

Eating disorders are treatable. Based on the individual case, hospitalization, outpatient treatment, and/or medication may be indicated. In addition, individual, family, and group therapy address the emotional, psychological, and social causes of the eating disorder. Family therapy helps family members develop more effective communication styles and create a safe atmosphere in which the child can express feelings, enhancing the success of recovery.

"The body is the soul's house. Shouldn't we therefore take care of our house so that it doesn't fall into ruin?" asked Philo Judaeus of Alexandria 2,000 years ago.[1] To develop healthy attitudes about appearance and eating in our children, we first need to take care of the souls in their bodies.

Building Healthy Body Image

1. If your life feels too hectic, arrange your schedule to be more available to your children. Set aside dinner time as family time, for example. A good way to begin is Shabbat dinner.

2. Ask your synagogue youth group leader, school principal, or camp director to arrange an educational program on body image and eating through Jewish Family Services or another resource.

3. Avoid seeking someone to blame if your child develops an eating disorder. Get treatment quickly and work together as a family toward healing and recovery.

---

[1]Philo Judaeus, *The Worse Attacks the Better*, section 10, cited in Francine Klagsbrun, *Voices of Wisdom: Jewish Ideals and Ethics for Everyday Living*, Middle Village, NY: Jonathan David Publishers, Inc., p. 210.

Is It Love or Is It Spoiling?

Here's a little checklist for the modern parent. Does your child ask you to buy something for him every time you go into a store? Do you feel compelled to buy what he requests? Are there times when you give your child treats or toys when she doesn't ask for them? How do you react when your child whines or loses her temper because she isn't getting her way? Does your child ever fail to express gratitude when you've done something special for him?

These situations and dilemmas are not unique to today's parents. "Pamper a child and he will shock you," warned Ben Sira, who wrote a book of proverbs in Jerusalem around 200 B.C.E. The Babylonian Talmud (tractate Ta'anit) gives a colorful description of what we'd surely label a spoiled child: "a son who acts petulantly before his father and he grants his wishes; so that if the son says to him, 'Bathe me in warm water,' the father bathes him in warm water; 'Wash me in cold water,' he washes him in cold water; 'Give me nuts, peaches, almonds and pomegranates,' he gives him nuts, peaches, almonds and pomegranates." (According to Rabbi Menachem Goldberger of Tiferes Yisroel Congregation, this portrait is used to illustrate the special relationship that Honi, "the Circle Maker," achieved with God. Because of Honi's exceptional piety, God granted his requests—for example, by ending a drought. The story makes the point that, outside such a context, a child is not entitled to this kind of special treatment.)

What exactly does "spoiling" a child mean, and is it necessarily bad? The very term suggests doing something undesirable, even harmful. The dictionary defines "spoil" in human relationships as "impairing in character or disposition by unwise treatment or benefits, especially by excessive indulgence." Spoiling is something an adult does *to* a child, with consequences affecting the child, the adult, and others around them.

A good starting point for a discussion of spoiling is our understanding of human nature. Judaism views children as a blessing; the very first *mitzvah* (commandment) is "Be fruitful and multiply." Judaism teaches that "at the core, a human being is good and pure," says Rabbi Goldberger. "The essence of the human being is one thing, but the development of character is another," he continues. "Not until Bar/Bat Mitzvah is the child considered to have developed mature knowledge, responsibility, and understanding of the consequences of behavior. The parent's job is to help the child develop and grow in this direction."

"Spoiling" a child usually involves either (or both) *giving* and *giving in*, to an excessive extent. We give our children material things, and often they are given these things for little or no effort on their part. Their needs are immediately gratified, so that they don't have to wait for things they want. When they ask us, push us, nag us, or get angry at us, we may give in and say, in effect, "Have your way."

As parents, we need to look at the motives and values behind our behavior with our children. Why are we giving and giving in, how much are we doing it, and how are our children being affected?

Parents give to their children for a whole range of reasons. To create an incentive for a child, or to reward him for something desirable he has done, is often a perfectly valid reason for giving. For example, promising an ice cream cone to a three-year-old who hates getting a haircut may enable him to exert enough self-control to tolerate the unpleasant experience. It is not likely to create a lifelong expectation of a tangible reward for good behavior if the parent helps him to develop self-control as he matures.

It is natural for parents whose opportunities and possessions were limited when they were young to want their children to have more. However, some give unstintingly to their children, even exceeding their actual financial resources. Others give—or give in—because of feelings of guilt. Parents whose work schedules leave them little time to spend with their children may compensate by lavishing things on them. The desire to compensate may also be connected to a child's disability. For example, some families today may relate to this account by Rabbi Judah ben Asher of Toledo, who was born in 1270: "Now because of the weakness of my eyesight [in childhood], my father and mother left me to do whatever was right in my own eyes; they never punished or rebuked me. Wherefore I have never been wont to chide others; for they taught me not how, even my own sons I knew not how to reprove."

Another reason that parents give so much to children is that they are subject to constant pressure from the mass media. This pervasive commercialism affects children, too, as is readily evident in the TV ads accompanying children's cartoon shows. Parents also feel pressure to "keep up with the Joneses," which their children may, in turn, convey to them by assuring their parents that "Everyone else has . . ." whatever new thing they desire. These social pressures thrive on feelings of inadequacy, envy, and competition. Wanting their children to look up to them and feel they have power, parents may use money and ownership of things to achieve that sense of importance.

Finally, some parents simply cannot tolerate a child's frustration or anger. They may be too stressed, tired, or distracted by other responsibilities to deal with these reactions. Teaching self-control takes time and effort; it is simpler just to keep the child quiet by buying what he wants or giving in to another request.

Although many of these reactions and feelings are natural, parents need to ask whether they may be harming the child. What messages does a child get if the parent buys him something every time they go into a store or accedes to every whined entreaty? The kind of spoiling that is negative, says Rabbi Goldberger, is the unnecessary showering of things, resulting in a child's thinking that everything is coming to him. This interferes with the child's development of responsibility. An indicator of spoiling, he says, is "if a parent observes an unhealthy lack of appreciation of what effort means, or of the parent's expenditure of time and energy."

Children who value only *getting* may not learn the importance of empathy for others, of responding to the giver and understanding that someone cared enough to give them a gift or do something for them. They may also have so many possessions, acquired with no effort, that they don't learn the value of work and earning money. Even by their own buying behavior, parents may be modelling this kind of spoiling. How many of us get excited about and buy new products or clothes, only to use them briefly or not at all?

There is a kind of spoiling that is more subtle than giving or giving in. Another proverb from the "Wisdom of Ben Sira" says, "A man who spoils his son will bandage every wound and will be on tenterhooks at every cry." The over-protective parent is not helping his child learn to be self-reliant.

Spoiling works against the development of competence. The more a child participates in getting what he wants, the more a sense of self-esteem will accompany getting what he gets.

Two other kinds of relationships in which spoiling sometimes occurs involve siblings and grandparents. The Babylonian Talmud cautions that "a man should never single out one son among his others, for on account of [the coat of many colors] that Jacob gave Joseph in excess of his other sons, his brothers became jealous of him, and the matter resulted in our forefathers' exile in Egypt." Favoritism toward one child over another can have grave consequences within families to this day.

While the special relationship between grandparents and grandchildren allows for a little laxness and indulgence, "some grandparents abuse their license" by ignoring the parents' rules or buying expensive gifts for their grandchildren, says Arthur Kornhaber, M.D. in *Between Parents and Grandparents*. He points out that "when spoiling is intertwined with family competitiveness, a youngster can become the prize in a major competition. Parents feel undermined and become diminished in the eyes of their children. . . . An adversarial system between parents and grandparents can be avoided by a wise and understanding grandparent."

Ultimately, you want to be valued by your child (or grandchild) for *who you are and what you have to offer in a relationship*. If parents can focus on the goal of teaching children the value of relationships, they are less likely to use spoiling behavior. "Some of the most special things parents can give their children are those that can't be measured quantitatively; they are the things we give of ourselves," says Rachel Meisels, who coordinates Judaic family programming and teaches in the Goldsmith Early Childhood Education Center at Chizuk Amuno Congregation.

A perfect example of this kind of giving is reading together, which Mrs. Meisels describes as "a special, private time for closeness and cuddling between parent and child, ideally in a relaxed, unthreatening, and uninterrupted setting." Through regular reading with a parent, a child can acquire confidence about decision-making (by choosing which stories to read) and a sense of mastery (from re-reading favorite stories and even learning some parts by heart). In addition, a story can help a parent find out how a child feels about something (such as a certain fear), thus opening the door to communication. When young children gain a pleasurable association from reading, they can turn to books for pleasure and knowledge throughout life.

Self-confidence, self-reliance, the ability to find one's own inner resources, responsibility, and the enjoyment of relationships—these are all values we want to teach our children—and we can, by not spoiling them.

How to Avoid Spoiling a Child

1. Look at your child as a unique individual. Understand and help him see what truly interests him. If he loves soccer, ask, "Do you really want/need that hockey stick?" Or "I notice you enjoy your train set most of all."

2. Personalize gifts so they are appropriate to each child's interests and needs. You do not have to spend exactly the same amount for each child in the family.

3. Consider ways to reward desirable behavior other than by giving material things. These can include hugs, verbal praise, and emphasizing the child's own satisfaction in a job well-done or in helping others and seeing how good it makes them feel.

4. Share with your child the experience of looking forward to something and working or saving money toward a goal, such as a family trip. For a young child who needs to see results quickly, baking challah for Shabbat together is a process accomplished in one

day, with participation in each stage and delicious results. Another wonderful family activity for parents and children of any age is planting and caring for a garden, and then reaping the fruits.

5. Focus on *your* family: your resources, values, and unique family experiences.

To Tell or Not to Tell?

Do you enjoy sharing memories of your earlier years with your children? When do you focus on the pleasant memories, and when do the sad ones surface? Are there parts of your past that you feel hesitant to discuss with your children?

Judaism places strong emphasis on remembering. Every year we retell the Passover story at the seder. We talk about both the good and the bad parts of our history. Yom Hashoah is to ensure that we never forget the most awful modern chapter, the Holocaust. We observe Yom Hazikaron, the Day of Remembrance for those who fell in the struggles to establish and defend the State of Israel. The Yizkor prayers recall those beloved to us who have died. On Yom Kippur, we are told that God remembers *all* our deeds of the past year, which we ourselves must review. Other examples of both collective and personal remembering abound—and they can speak to our experience as parents.

Children are naturally curious about their parents' earlier lives. Most parents like telling their children about themselves, so that they can feel more connected and better understand what experiences shaped them, says child psychologist Bruno Bettelheim in *A Good Enough Parent*.

It's easy to share our good memories. But parents struggle with what, and how much, to tell about the more painful parts of our pasts. Some of the experiences affecting us before our children knew us might include: sexual abuse in childhood, substance abuse (drugs or alcohol), arrest, premarital sex, divorce, infertility, or the loss of a child. Whether these were things that we *did* or things that *happened* to us, they are not easy subjects to talk about, even adult to adult.

If ever there was a person with a painful past, it was Joseph, whose story is one of the most powerful and fully developed in the Bible. Indulged by his father and visited by divine dreams, he lorded it over his brothers, until they conspired to kill him. They stripped him of his beautiful coat and cast him into a pit. Only through the intervention of his brother Judah did he escape death, being sold instead to some passing merchants. And so Joseph, at age 17, arrived in Egypt, a miserable slave.

The Bible relates Joseph's subsequent rise to the Pharoah's favor, his public prominence and wealth. As Viceroy of the land, he is given an Egyptian name and marries an Egyptian woman, with whom he has two sons.

Some intriguing questions present themselves as we read this story. What were Joseph's feelings when his sons were born? Did he think of his own family, with whom his connection was so brutally and abruptly severed? Was he able to close off that part of his life and view his experience in Egypt as a completely new and separate chapter? Did he ever think of telling his wife or his sons about his previous life? Did Joseph, the dreamer and famous interpreter of dreams, ever dream about his past? Did he unwittingly reveal elements of his past by talking in his sleep?

In fact, both the Torah and commentaries on this dramatic story address some of these questions. They hold many insights for us today as we struggle with difficult aspects of our own pasts. It is striking to learn that Joseph names his first son Menasheh, literally, "making to forget," because, as he explains, "God has made me forget all my toil and everything in my father's house." (Genesis 41:51) The Talmud explains that "It was the custom to name children according to the events of one's life. If the name recalls an unpleasant incident, it is a reminder to praise God for letting the person escape the evil." (*Shemot Rabbah*)

However, it is clear that Joseph has forgotten none of his previous life when his brothers arrive in Egypt years later in search of food because of a famine in Canaan. Now a mature man, Joseph recognizes them immediately, while the brothers haven't a clue as to his real identity, so changed is he. Joseph proceeds to invent an elaborate series of manipulative ploys (accusing his brothers of being spies and stealing from him, imprisoning them, and sending them back home to bring his youngest brother Benjamin to him). All of this is done as a test to see if, after 22 years of separation, his brothers have changed, repented their evil deeds, and can feel affection for him, says Rabbi Yaakov Culi, the Sephardic sage (1689–1732) who wrote *MeAm Lo'ez*, a collection of commentaries woven into Biblical stories.

What is fascinating is how Joseph *uses* elements of his past in this process, convincing the brothers that he has "mystical powers" because he knows their names and the most intimate details of their home life. Joseph also uses his son Menasheh as a key player in these interactions with his brothers, according to the medieval commentator Rashi and the *midrash*. We are left to imagine how Joseph's Egyptian family reacted to his revelation of his true identity and history.

The family dilemmas and dynamics in this ancient story resound for a modern audience. The Bible seems to be saying not only that we cannot forget our past lives, but they have meaning in our present ones. By integrating lessons from *then* into *now*, we can move forward in a healthy way. And how we deal with our past does affect how we parent our children.

Adults have a right to privacy—as do children. It's up to you to decide what information to communicate to your children and when. "All emotionally loaded situations . . . have the potential for both good and bad," says Dr. Bettelheim. Telling a child about the past can bring you closer, he continues, *if* it is done with care. Be aware of your own feelings and motives, and think about how the telling will affect your child.

If a parent tells the child about an earlier traumatic experience, the child may feel guilty for having a better life, or for causing the parent more hurt, Dr. Bettelheim points out. Children see their own acts as having a far greater impact on their parents than, in fact, they do. When parents divorce, for example, children need to be reassured that they did not cause the break-up, says Joan Kristall, director of Jewish Family Services' Programs for Families of Separation, Divorce, and Remarriage.

Parents may avoid discussing difficult periods in their history simply because it is too painful for them. Also, they wish to shield their children from distressing realities. However, secrecy can cause a child much anxiety and suffering. The child picks up on her parent's reticence—and blames herself. In *Living After the Holocaust: Reflections by Children of Survivors in America*, Dr. Lucy Y. Steinitz, whose German-born parents told her nothing during her childhood of their horrible experiences during World War II, had to reconstruct their lives. "I tried to imagine myself in their position: would I have had the courage to go on? They had proven their stamina, their bravery, their heroism; I had not, could not, do the same." This is another effect of parental secrecy pointed out by Dr. Bettelheim: it can undermine the child's confidence in her ability to overcome difficulties in her own life.

We need to seek a balance between protecting our children from the harshness of life, and giving them information enabling them to deal with life's realities. In deciding what to tell about yourself and when, whether to volunteer information, or wait for the child to ask, consider the following variables: the child's age and developmental level, his maturity, his individual personality, and the kind of relationship you have with him. The decision about what to reveal at age 4 will be quite different from what to say at age 12, and there may be many tellings.

It is also vital to examine your motives for communicating the information at this time. Are you trying to make the child feel grateful for what you have done for him, or to make him more considerate of you? "When I was a child, I had to walk four miles back and forth to school every day. Do you know how lucky you are to be taken door to door by a bus?" Do you perhaps feel some envy of your child's easier life, and bitterness that you had to go through difficult times? Many of us are not conscious of these feelings, but they can color how we talk to our children.

"Most parents find it hard to realize that it is nearly impossible for a child to appreciate 'advantages' in regard to which he had no choice," says Dr. Bettelheim. Look at things from the child's perspective. He may define "hardship" quite differently than a parent does: his definition may include doing chores or homework, or having a younger sibling. Remember that today's world has different realities from the world in which we grew up.

Try to avoid presenting facts in a negative way: "I wish I'd never met my first husband" or "It was the worst thing I ever went through" or "I was such a troublemaker in Hebrew School." Instead, use these opportunities helpfully, to teach good values and basic truths: behavior has consequences; even parents are fallible; we can learn from our mistakes; we change and grow; we can find resources inside and outside ourselves to deal with adversity.

One of the things adults struggle with is whether we can ever put the past completely behind us. Time does heal wounds, but scars remain. All of our experiences become part of us and affect who we are, and it's OK to let our children know that. How can we present the unflattering or painful parts of our history in a way that is not self-serving, in a way our child can understand?, asks Rabbi Donald Berlin of Temple Oheb Shalom. "He shouldn't have to hear it from someone else; it's part of his history and it's a way to understand who he is. The important question is: 'What is the legacy that I want to leave?'"

In a beautiful Biblical scene, Jacob blesses all his sons before his death. He adopts Joseph's sons, Ephraim and Menasheh, as his own and blesses Joseph through them, thereby reinforcing the family link that was broken so many years before. Menasheh and his brother can be seen as symbols of the relationship between forgetting and remembering. It is a custom for Jewish fathers to bless their children every Friday night, saying, "May God make you like Ephraim and Menasheh." Rashi comments that "These few words include all the blessings in the world."

Tips About Telling

1. If your child asks a question, find out what he really wants to know. Go slowly; he may not want or need *all* the information at that time.

2. If a question catches you off guard, explain that it's an important question, and you need to give yourself some time to think about it before answering.

3. Information that is very painful can be imparted in a generalized, rather than a personal, way ("Many people feel that . . ." "That was a painful time in Jewish history . . .")

4. Many resources are available to help you clarify these issues, including social workers, rabbis, school personnel, and support groups.

5. If you are not comfortable sharing a part of your past with your child now, or worry that you may never feel able to talk about it, you could write an account of it and put it away in a safe place for your child to read at a designated age.

6. And don't forget to share the good memories: childhood stories can be told and retold, in person and even on tape.

Falling Stars and Earthly Models

He is "ruddy-cheeked with beautiful eyes, and handsome," "skilled in music, a mighty man and a fighter, and sensible in speech." "Successful in all his undertakings . . . his reputation soars." One of his fans tells him, "No wrong is ever to be found in you."

Does this sound like the portrait of a familiar contemporary idol? Who is this man whose physical prowess is matched by his intellectual and creative powers—the perfect hero, to his adoring followers?

This is the Biblical description of the young David (from the first book of *Samuel*), catapulted to fame by his victory over the Philistine Goliath, and chosen by God to become king of his people. But the accomplishments and traits for which David was beloved are the same ones that attract many of us to public figures today.

Contemporary popular darlings include athletes, movie actors, musicians. "Ripken in Galaxy of [His] Own Amid Stars," read a 1994 headline in the Baltimore *Sun*, which dubbed the Baltimore Orioles shortstop "one of baseball's living legends."[1] Cal Ripken, Jr., went on to break Lou Gehrig's record of 2,130 consecutive games played. Reflecting national adulation and the fans' "yearning for true heroes," Ripken was *Sports Illustrated*'s choice for the 1995 Sportsman of the Year.

The problem is that celebrities can let us down. Questions about personal morality have tarnished presidents, popular singers, and many other public personalities. In 1994, figure skater Tonya Hard-

---

[1] *The Evening Sun*, Baltimore, MD, July 12, 1994.

ing met disgrace through her suspected participation in a plot that injured Olympic teammate, Nancy Kerrigan. In the same year, football star O.J. Simpson was charged with murdering his ex-wife, Nicole Brown, and her friend, Ronald L. Goldman. The Simpson criminal trial mesmerized the country for months, with the fascination continuing even after a jury acquitted him.

How are parents to explain these events to children? How can we help our kids deal with their sense of betrayal when public figures they revere fall off their pedestals? How can we guide children to decide which people are worthy of their admiration and emulation?

All of us—children and adults—need people to admire. We need role models, real people close to us who set examples of the way we'd like to live—goals we feel are attainable. And we also need heroes to inspire us, people whose greatness makes us dream and expands our vision beyond ourselves.

How do we choose these figures? The first role models children encounter are their parents, or other immediate caregivers. Young children think concretely, so they naturally esteem physical strength and other characteristics they can see in their parents and other adults. They are also influenced in these early years by the views they hear their parents express.

In addition, a child's own personality, interests, and gender affect his or her choices of people to admire. From about age 8 continuing into adolescence, the influence of peers becomes very significant.

Finally, the media have a tremendous impact on children's views of popular figures, often sensationalizing both their achievements and failures. It is almost impossible for celebrities today to have private lives. Imagine what television, talk shows, and tabloids would have done with King David's early rise to fame and his military exploits. How they would have revelled in exposing his subsequent intrigues, sins, and personal losses!

By bringing celebrities into our homes, the media create a superficial sense of intimacy. Children feel they *know* their superstars. It takes insight and some maturity to distinguish the person inside from the gloss, to realize that all they know is what the media show.

What parents can do is to help their children develop realistic views and expectations of the famous people they admire. Like King

David, public figures today are not perfect. They are imperfect human beings, some of whom have reached great heights in certain areas. Rabbi Mark Loeb of Beth El Congregation recalls being in his twenties and seeing a famous actor give a brilliant performance. When the young fan went backstage after the play to ask the actor for his autograph, the celebrity splattered him with verbal abuse. From this painful encounter, says Rabbi Loeb, "I learned that talent is not a barometer of character."

Thus, parents need to tell young children that just because a person has a beautiful face, strong body, or a certain gift, we can't assume that he or she is a *mensch*, a good person. Being a celebrity does not automatically make one a hero or a role model. A valid admiration for another person is built on knowledge of the area in which he or she excels.

At the heart of the matter are values. Beginning when a child is around age 7 or 8, parents can pose questions such as, "What children do you like being friends with? What's special about these friends? What adults do you respect and why?" Through specific examples drawn from their personal relationships, like "Sammy helped me get up when I fell," or "Sarah works the hardest at soccer practice," the child learns to identify qualities such as compassion, generosity, and effort.

Parents can also help their children by teaching them about heroic figures that reflect Jewish values. The Bible and Talmud are filled with fascinating personalities who can become Jewish heroes to children of all ages. By reading Biblical and Rabbinic stories to our children and discussing the Jewish heroes described in them, we can guide children to develop an appreciation for Judaism's unique understanding of what a true hero really is. Whether they are ancient Jewish heroes like Abraham, Sarah, Moses, Miriam, David, Esther, Judith, Rabbi Akiva, Beruria and Judah Maccabee—or more contemporary figures such as David Ben-Gurion, Hannah Senesh, Golda Meir, Jonathan Netanyahu and Natan and Avital Sharansky, Jewish heroes can help children build pride and confidence in their Jewishness while reinforcing the values that have made our heroes so important to Jewish continuity.

Ben Zoma taught: "Who is a hero? One who conquers his passion, as it is written, 'One who is slow to anger is better than a hero, and one who rules over his spirit [better] than he who conquers a city.'" (Proverbs 16:32) The Hebrew word for "hero" is *gibbor,* whose root is "strength." This teaching from *Pirke Avot* (*Ethics of the Fathers* 4:1) presents the ideal hero, although many historical Jewish figures labelled heroic actually did not possess the self-restraint that Ben Zoma urged, says Rabbi Jack Moline in *Jewish Leadership and Heroism*.

Commenting on Ben Zoma's explanation, Rabbi Moline cites Rabbi Jonah ben Abraham Gerondi, who lived in the thirteenth century. Rabbi Jonah noted that human beings and animals both possess physical strength, but only humans have "spiritual strength." Ben Zoma's teaching refers to the latter, an "inner strength" [*gevurat ha-lev*, strength of the heart] . . . the strength to conquer one's passions," said Rabbi Jonah.

Thus, concludes Rabbi Moline's study of these two texts, "the greatest type of heroism is that which is considered, reasoned and controlled—not at all impulsive. . . . Circumstances and opportunity play as much a role in heroism as the character of the hero. . . . When circumstances present themselves, heroes respond more often than not out of a certain wisdom gained through experience, wisdom which has become so much a part of themselves that their response is almost a reflex."

A case in point is Aaron Feuerstein, owner of the Malden Mills factory in Methuen, Massachusetts, a third-generation family business producing the thermal fabric Polartec. When the factory burned down in December 1995, Mr. Feuerstein promised to rebuild locally and to hire back as many employees as possible. Meanwhile, workers were assured of their full salaries for at least a month, and everyone received a Christmas bonus.

For this, Massachusetts Governor William F. Weld called Mr. Feuerstein "a great American hero," and the story received national attention. The owner's actions were seen as extraordinary in an era of corporate "downsizing" and layoffs—a time when more and more employers show no such loyalty to their workers. When asked why he took these steps to protect his employees, Mr. Feuerstein, an Orthodox Jew, quoted a teaching from Hillel that he had learned from his father: "When all is moral chaos, this is the time for you to be a *mensch*."

"Heroes . . . reflect the values of a society," says Rabbi Jack Moline. Commenting on this event, syndicated columnist Ellen Goodman lamented the fact that the decency and loyalty which Aaron Feuerstein showed his employees are considered exceptional today. Goodman found a "moral message for the competitive world" in this story: "This is all it takes to be a hero: be a mensch."[1]

Such a definition is far from the description of King David at the beginning of this discussion. But Mr. Feuerstein's story presents a view of heroism that can have a significant impact on children.

Another approach to teaching values for discerning worthy role models is to encourage children to look inside to identify the qualities they like and respect in themselves—and then to find others in whom they recognize these qualities. This process builds self-esteem as well as a healthy basis of admiration for others. When parents listen to what their children value, helping them articulate what they think is important, children learn to trust their own judgment and will be better prepared to withstand outside pressures in adolescence.

Teenagers from ages 12 to 14 are especially prone to infatuations with and idealization of public figures, prior to their preoccupation with the opposite sex, notes teacher Geoffrey Basik, assistant director for Secondary Education at the Council on Jewish Education Services (CJES). He says parents can encourage children of Bar or Bat Mitzvah age to consider: "What kind of person do I want to be when I grow up? What do I want to do with my life? What's worthy of emulation in the people I admire? Is it wealth and fame, or the discipline, hard work, and other character traits required to get there? Is heroism doing one act, or is it the kind of person someone is?" The definition of a real model, says Basik, is "one who makes us think, 'I can be like that.' The central question is how to apply these lofty ideals to our lives."

Basik also suggests that parents and educators identify values they consider important, and then help children find models who exemplify them. Judaism presents us with many embodiments of virtues

---

[1] *The Sun*, Baltimore, MD, December 22, 1995

like hospitality, honesty, and *tzedakah*, he says. Mill owner Aaron Feuerstein is one such example.

We can also point out people in the larger world who practice values important in Judaism. In an article called "Ripken as a Role Model,"[1] Baltimore Orioles fan Gary Rosenblatt, editor of *The Jewish Week* of New York and former editor of the *Baltimore Jewish Times*, reflects that "In embracing Cal Ripken, as so many fans have, we are almost palpably pining for the simpler times when heroes really were heroic and when cynicism was not so pervasive." Rosenblatt thinks Talmudic scholar Rabbi Tarfon "would have loved Cal Ripken, Jr." Why? Ripken embodies Rabbi Tarfon's teaching in *Pirke Avot* (*Ethics of the Fathers* 2:20–21): "The day is short, the task is abundant, the laborers are lazy, the wage is great, and the Master is insistent. You are not required to complete the task, yet you are not free to withdraw from it." Rosenblatt comments that "Ripken comes to remind us that there are no short-cuts to long-term success . . . [and that] our task is not to perform miracles but to keep our focus and do our own little bit, one day at a time. . . ."

Parents still need to acknowledge and deal with their children's responses when the stars they revere fall from the heights. Using empathy helps children with their feelings of shock, confusion, and disappointment. "I can understand why it's hard to imagine someone you admire could do something awful." By acknowledging the child's feelings, parents can help him begin to deal with the reality that sometimes people *do* let us down.

These questions are not new. How could a man like King David, who wrote such beautiful poetry, we might ask, plot the death of the husband of Bathsheba, a woman he wanted? It helps to let children know that adults, too, are deeply perplexed when a public figure they admire does immoral things in other parts of his or her life.

At the same time, we need to make it clear that certain acts *are* awful. Spouse or child abuse, physical attacks, cheating, even unsportsmanlike behavior are not excusable for anyone, famous or not. These incidents can serve as opportunities for family reflection and discussion.

---

[1]*Baltimore Jewish Times*, September 8, 1995

Keeping a sense of balance is important. We do not want to make children disillusioned, cynical, or fearful. Yes, there are some people who do bad things, but there are also many who are worthy of our admiration. Judaism recognizes the complexity of human nature, teaching that we all have the potential for doing evil as well as good. In Psalm 24, King David said it all: "Who may ascend the mountain of the Lord? . . . He who has clean hands and a pure heart . . ." One of our jobs as parents is to guide our children to find people who can inspire them, by virtue of their values and character, to develop the best in themselves.

Where Have All the Heroes Gone? Suggestions for Parents

1. Encourage children to look for ordinary people—adults and peers—in their own community who are doing extraordinary things they admire. Start a family bulletin board with newspaper clippings about such people.

2. Children need to see who their parents' heroes are, says CJES' Geoffrey Basik. This takes some introspection, and it makes a good basis for a family discussion about values. Include Jewish heroic figures in your discussions.

3. A great opportunity to highlight Jewish heroic figures is on Sukkot, when a different Biblical person is traditionally invited to visit the sukkah and sit with us each night. This ritual of extending hospitality is called *ushpizin*.

4. Urge children to discuss their feelings with someone they know and respect, like a rabbi or a teacher, when people they admire disappoint them.

5. Teach children that they can make significant contributions by doing even small acts of *tzedakah* in everyday life at home and in the community.

Holidays and Seasons

Making the High Holidays Meaningful for Children

What do the High Holidays mean to a child? Eating apples dipped in honey, wearing a new suit or dress, getting together with family, seeing large crowds in synagogue, and hearing the Shofar all give children opportunities to participate in the holidays. However, children sometimes feel excluded if they are not praying for hours in services or fasting as adults do. They are curious about what adults are doing and why.

Parents may find it a challenge to convey the profound message of Rosh Hashanah and Yom Kippur to children. However, children do sense the special excitement and solemnity of the "Days of Awe." Parents can enhance their child's understanding of and involvement in the holidays, if they themselves decide what they want to teach and gear it to the child's developmental level.

Rosh Hashanah and Yom Kippur are about growth and changing, and about community. Children can grasp both of these concepts if they are presented in concrete ways. "Saul, what can you do this year that you couldn't do last year? You can ride a two-wheel bike. You can read a Hebrew prayer." "Julie, try squeezing into the dress you wore last Rosh Hashanah. Look how tall you grew!" Parents can take their children into the synagogue, pointing out that the Torah covers have been changed to white instead of the usual purple or blue. Let children participate in opening and sending New Year's cards.

More problematic for many parents are the ideas of sin and repentance. Looking at the Hebrew words for these ideas gives us a better base of understanding for communicating with children. Hebrew has several words translated as "sin," reflecting a range of seriousness in behavior and several types of relationships involved. One of these, *chait*, literally means "to miss the mark." You are aiming for a goal and you don't get it, so you try again. Sins can be described as "mistakes or missed opportunities" to do something which would have made us better people, says Rabbi Harold S. Kushner, author of *When Children Ask About God*.

The Hebrew word for repentance is *teshuvah* (meaning "to return"). The *chait* is straying from the path where you wanted to go, and the *teshuvah* is getting yourself back on the path. The idea of *teshuvah* is to grow into what you would like to be. Remorse about past mistakes becomes the motivator for growth.

Can children grasp these ideas, and how much should parents discuss with them? The answers depend on a child's age and mental and emotional readiness. Between the ages of 3 and 6, children begin to develop a conscience. They are still very dependent on their parents' views of right and wrong and on the pressure of adult authority to comply. Elementary school-age children's ideas about right and wrong begin to be influenced by experiences in school and with their peers. Adult rules are seen as immutable, but they have no ethical value or significance to children. Many children this age see God as a magnified parent. They start to develop an inner control that points out right versus wrong, but children do not make a distinction between doing something adults label "bad" or "good" and being a "bad" or "good" *person*. Therefore, it is important for parents to choose their language carefully according to the child's age and developmental level.

Adolescents become more capable of logical thinking and introspection, and they can assess their behavior as it relates to ideals. They are struggling with who they want to be in this world. Kushner points out that "the development of the idea of God as an outside voice of authority into . . . an internalized voice of commitment and conscience terminates a long process of maturation. . . ."

One aspect of *chait* which we can handle with young children is the idea of not doing something perfectly, because this is part of their normal life process. Children realize they do not yet have all the skills they need. Grown-ups, too, are always learning and improving. Stress the positives with children: we learn and grow from our mistakes. In what ways would we like to change our behavior? How can we do better next time?

Parents can communicate the value of *teshuvah* without invoking the image of an angry, demanding God who will punish us if we do not act properly, says Rabbi David J. Wolpe of the University of Judaism in Los Angeles, California. "It is far better to teach that our actions, good and bad, are important because we are important"[1]— important to other people and to God. Feeling this connection to God can encourage in children the development of an inner sense of improving and growing.

Wolpe stresses that parents need not have all the answers in order to talk with their children; we can begin simply "by creating an atmosphere receptive to discussion of spiritual questions and spiritual quests." Encouraging children to express their feelings verbally is the first step in helping them learn how to handle feelings and how to change constructively.

Adults recite communal confessions (*Al Chet, Avinu Malkenu*) on the High Holidays. It is important that children of all ages feel that they, too, are a part of the community, and that their actions affect who the Jewish people are. Although the very young child is egocentered, as he grows he begins to get a sense of himself as a family member, then as a member of a peer group, and finally as a part of a larger community. Including children in the holiday nurtures this sense of belonging.

The High Holidays, for adults and children alike, are opportunities to stop and think about how we are going to grow this year, so that we can look back and say we have really changed in ways that we wanted to change. The key to children's participation in this pro-

---

[1]David J. Wolpe, "Letting God In," *Hadassah Magazine*, August/September 1992, pp. 42–43.

cess is first to make *teshuvah* concrete. As children mature, their understanding of the concept will deepen.

Suggestions for Introducing the Concept of Teshuvah to Children

1. It is not realistic to expect children to sit for long periods in services. However, if it is possible to arrange, bring your children into the adult service at a prime time such as when the Shofar is blown. Explain to them that they are part of the whole community that is sharing this moment. If your children remain in the adult service for any length of time, give them books about the holidays appropriate to their level so they feel they are participating meaningfully.

2. To stress the theme of change, start a new kind of growth chart for your child, recording the acquisition of new skills, such as learning how to swim, how to write one's name in Hebrew, etc.

3. Help your child do *teshuvah* in a concrete way. Start by asking the child to talk about what she is sorry for and would like to change. "I would like to be able to share a special toy with another child." "I would like to do my chores without being reminded." Then help your child make a plan enabling her to reach her goal through practical small steps. "I will let Jon hold my bear next time for 5 minutes." "I will make my bed before I go down to breakfast so I won't forget." The goals should be reasonable and success-oriented; the child should be able to measure her progress. For example, rather than "I'm going to love my little brother even though he bothers me," the child can decide, "Instead of hitting him when he bothers me, I'm going to leave the room."

4. When a child has an awareness of having hurt another person through his actions, it is important for him to set the relationship straight by going directly to the person he has wronged. When a child says "I'm sorry" because he really feels for another person, the child is not just mouthing words; he understands that he is taking responsibility for the consequences of his behavior.

5. Adults have a tremendous impact as role models for children. One child was deeply impressed when he heard that his parent went to her sibling's home before Rosh Hashanah to try to end a long-standing quarrel. Also, a parent gives a powerful message when he does not feel demeaned by apologizing to a child: "I'm sorry I broke my promise to you" or "I'm sorry I lost my temper when you didn't deserve it."

Of Turkey and Tension:
Parents and Children at
Holiday Time

For weeks, Grandma Rose has been eagerly awaiting the arrival of her daughter's family for Thanksgiving. As the local relatives gather in her Baltimore home, Grandma puts the finishing touches on her traditional turkey, sweet potato kugel (a secret recipe no one has ever duplicated), cranberry relish, apple strudel, and all the other trimmings. Meanwhile, having left Cleveland before dawn, Sue and Paul are bogged down in a traffic jam. Two hours later, the out-of-towners stagger in, children cranky from lack of sleep and constant bickering, parents frazzled and wondering why they undertake this journey every year. Already upset about her dried-out dinner, Grandma takes one look at her grandson and says to her daughter, "Couldn't you find time to get his hair cut?" Her anticipation of the family reunion having dissolved hours before, Sue can only think, "How Mom has aged!"

Because home is the heart of Thanksgiving, it highlights family frictions—especially between parents and children—that surface when families come together for a brief, intense time. These tensions may arise during other holidays as well, but Thanksgiving is the most travelled American holiday, and one that Jews celebrate as whole-heartedly as their fellow citizens of all faiths, as Mordecai M. Kaplan pointed out in *Judaism as a Civilization.*[1] Whether we go away to go home, or provide the home to which others return, we approach the holiday with expectations. Frequently, however, the reality disappoints us.

Tradition and change. That's what holidays are about. Families that have undergone divorce or remarriage are acutely aware of change at such times. Their dilemma is with whom to spend the holiday: which grandparents, which parents? Thanksgiving, like other holidays, can be very painful for the children. "I dread being caught in the middle of a tug of war between my Mom and Dad," confides Stephanie, age 10, whose parents have been divorced for two years.

Even traditional families experience holiday tensions. As children grow up and marry, some choose to spend the holidays with their in-laws, other relatives or friends. These decisions can lead to hurt feelings, especially when a parent views a holiday as hers or his, expecting grown children and grandchildren to be present every year. Barry Levinson's "Avalon" captured some of these issues in two contrasting Thanksgiving dinners at the beginning and end of the film. By the closing scene, the large, intergenerational family, whose complex relationships once animated the long table, has shrunk to the nuclear unit, isolated in the suburbs, communication replaced by a television screen.

Holidays mark our lives, making us aware of the passage of time, changes in ourselves and our children, and especially loss. Perhaps we insist on keeping the food the same each year because it is one element we can control, unlike all the other changes life brings. A traditional Thanksgiving dinner is a tangible expression of the nurturing we associate with home. As parents age and roles are reversed, families can preserve a sense of continuity by passing on the traditional menu.

Another kind of tradition that tends to resurface when families meet for holidays involves the ways siblings, now adults, related to one another as children. Competition for attention, who is the favorite child, who mediates arguments, and who cleans up are examples of other "traditions" that get passed on. Some of these old patterns get played out between adult siblings over their children.

---

[1]Mordecai M. Kaplan, *Judaism as a Civilization*, Philadelphia: The Jewish Publication Society of America, Reconstructionist Press, 1981, p. 344

Diane, age 33, says, "I hate to say this, but my brother's kid is a spoiled brat. I don't like my son being around him. His manners are atrocious, his whining gets on my nerves, and he ruins every family dinner by making a scene."

The wear and tear of holiday travel and entertaining can exacerbate parent-child tensions. It is helpful to maintain at least part of the family's normal routine. Parents can bring along a beloved toy or blanket for a child sleeping in an unfamiliar place. Occasions like Thanksgiving are especially demanding for women, who may need a little assistance with the children from other family members in the midst of their intense preparations.

What can be done to defuse holiday tensions and avoid disappointment? First, try preparing for Thanksgiving by thinking about your relationships with your parents and children, anticipating the conflicts that may arise when you come together. Holidays can be opportunities to let go of old, unproductive patterns of relating and create newer ones that better reflect our present lives. At the same time, traditions that are cherished by all can be reaffirmed.

Think also about the changes that have occurred in your life. Our ability to adjust to life's changes enables us to cope with them. If we fight change, tensions and feelings of loss build, preventing us from making needed life transitions. Healthy change means, for example, being open to new family members, accepting one's grown children as adults, deriving pleasure from grandchildren, and accepting more responsibility in the family as one's parents age.

Add a measure of tolerance to your holiday recipes. Parents, grandparents, children, and siblings who can accept each other as they are will enjoy more relaxed family gatherings. Some find it better to avoid known areas of conflict; others may discuss them openly, acknowledging their differences but reaffirming their love for each other. Be aware of your needs—whether to communicate privately with certain family members, or to have some time for solitude or relaxation—and build in time to satisfy them.

Finally, channel some of the energy fueling parent-child conflicts in a positive direction. Instead of focusing so much on the meal, which can become the playing field for hostilities, explore, as a family, the meaning of the holiday. Rabbi Daniel Lehmann says, "Of all the American secular holidays, Thanksgiving resonates most positively with Judaism. Coming soon after Sukkot, it continues the themes of thanks for nature's abundance and human freedoms. It is especially fitting for us, as Jews, to celebrate our rights and blessings in this country. Thanksgiving is also an appropriate time for Jews to address problems of hunger and homelessness in the general community. Giving thanks implies sharing with others."

Rabbi Ira Schiffer, formerly of Beth Am Synagogue in Baltimore and now a resident of Carmiel/Misgav in Israel, suggests creating family Thanksgiving rituals, like those of Passover, that "will remain imprinted on our children's memories, symbolizing the meaning of the holiday. These rituals could also highlight the pluralistic richness of American society and the shared value of democracy." When continuing old family traditions feels more burdensome than satisfying, create a new tradition—such as simply taking a walk or playing a game together after dinner.

Tips to Reduce Holiday Tensions

1. Stress the positives and commonly-held values in family relationships. Give thanks for what is working well. Consider making a commitment in advance to avoid known areas of dispute with other family members.

2. Be flexible about holiday celebration. When all members of a family cannot observe the holiday on the actual calendar day because of other family commitments, try having Thanksgiving at another time, such as Shabbat dinner.

3. Reach out to others in need through social action as a cooperative family unit. Donate food or a few hours of time to a Kosher Food Pantry or a soup kitchen; invite someone without local family to your home; attend a multi-cultural program on Thanksgiving day.

4. Control the amount of responsibility falling on a few by making Thanksgiving dinner a potluck meal. Encourage a family member who has not hosted a holiday dinner to do so, with help, if necessary.

5. If your family is dispersed or diminished through death or divorce, invite another family or friends to share the holiday.

The December Dilemma

It's that time of the year again! Long cold nights and blustery, wintry days. Drinking hot cocoa by the fire, while memories of other winter seasons float through our heads. It's the holiday season, bringing with it mixed feelings of excitement and confusion. This state of mind has been aptly named The December Dilemma.

For many Jewish families, this time of year is troublesome. Even in predominantly Jewish neighborhoods, some Jewish children feel enticed by the beautiful Christmas lights, the music, the idea of a Christmas tree to decorate and thoughts of unwrapping presents on Christmas day. Some parents find it hard to resist their children's wishes to celebrate along with their Christian neighbors. Christmas may make parents feel vulnerable, as it tugs on their childhood roots. Some parents remember their own feelings and want to fulfill their childhood wishes along with their children.

This time of year asks us to look into ourselves and come to terms with our beliefs. The process can be painful and confusing for both parent and child, particularly in non-traditional Jewish homes. In being asked to justify their behavior to their children, parents can avoid giving mixed messages by having a clear understanding of their family's boundaries. In fact, this season can be viewed as an opportunity for parents to teach and reinforce their beliefs, and to help children solidify their own religious identity.

When a family is rooted in the Jewish faith, celebrating Hanukkah and other Jewish holidays, the children will not feel the need to compete with the Christian world around them nor to compensate.

They will know that Hanukkah simply happens to fall in December, and that it is celebrated according to the Jewish calendar.

Children can proudly decorate their homes with Hanukkah symbols, sing songs, re-tell the Hanukkah story, eat the traditional latkes with applesauce and *soofganiyot* (jelly doughnuts) as in Israel. They will delight each night in lighting the Hanukkah menorah and will partake in the centuries old tradition, knowing that all over the world, Jewish families are doing the same.

Some families believe that Christmas can be celebrated as a secular holiday. They have Christmas trees in their homes, perhaps calling them Hanukkah bushes. But to do this is to distort reality and insult both Hanukkah and Christmas. The Christmas tree is not a national symbol, but a Christian one. The evergreen symbolizes the resurrection and immortality of Jesus, and the wood represents the cross on which Jesus was crucified. Although many people today are unaware of the origins of the Christmas tree, clouded in a mixture of fact and legend, Rabbi Roland B. Gittelsohn points to the irony of Jews embracing this Christian symbol.[1]

By imitating another religion, families are making a statement that their holiday doesn't measure up. It is important to teach children to express their feelings and to help them learn healthy coping skills, in order to tolerate jealousy or coveting something they cannot have. Values clarification is essential for understanding one's self and for developing a sense of identity, including religious identity.

During this holiday season, children can begin to recognize what is special about their holiday and can learn how their heritage is different and unique. December is one of the times of the year when Jewish children have the opportunity to explore what belonging to a minority in the American culture means to them. Parents can help their children develop a positive sense of identity as they grow by using occasions like the holidays for discussion and airing feelings.

Furthermore, as a well defined identity leads to a healthier sense of self, it enhances one's ability to relate positively to others. If children can learn to honor their own tradition, then they will grow to

---

[1]Cited in Warren and Rebecca Boroson, "Coping with Santa Claus," *Jewish Living*, Nov.–Dec. 1979, p. 32.

respect the practices of others. If we emphasize Christmas at the expense of our own history and culture, we deprive ourselves of a growing relationship with Judaism.

How do we cope with Christmas and Hanukkah in a positive way? It is important to join with other Jewish families facing similar dilemmas and experience the special feelings of being Jewish. All Jewish holidays, including Hanukkah, can be observed in a concrete, emotional and spiritual manner. By providing positive experiences all year long, there is likely to be less concern in December. Through family observance of the holidays year round, children do not feel left out at Christmas. Dr. Ron Wolfson, Director of the Shirley and Arthur Whizin Center and Institute for Jewish Family Life at the University of Judaism in Los Angeles, California, says in *The Art of Jewish Living: Hanukkah,* "The child who has paraded with the Torah on Simhat Torah, planted trees at Tu BiShvat, brought fresh fruits at Shavuot, given *mishlóach manot* at Purim, and welcomed the Shabbat weekly with candles and wine and challah by the time he/she is three years old will understand that to be Jewish is to be enriched by a calendar brimming with joyous celebration."

It's important to spend time together as a family, openly expressing feelings and actively living the family's belief system. This system is tested often all year round. But the job of Jewish parents may be even harder at this season. By reinforcing your own beliefs and providing consistent messages, you are educating your children and helping them identify with their family and their relationship to Judaism.

Defusing December Dilemmas

1. Parents dealing with December dilemmas "need to create guidelines and draw borders around their religious practices," says Dr. Ron Wolfson. Remember that Hanukkah celebrates the Maccabees' fight for religious freedom and "the right *not* to assimilate into the majority culture."

2. Avoid comparing Hanukkah to Christmas or presenting it to children as an alternative. We can respect and appreciate another's holiday, while making it clear that it is not "our" holiday.

3. Dr. Wolfson suggests that families can show their commitment to Jewish humanitarian values on Christmas Day by volunteering to help in shelters, soup kitchens, or necessary service jobs so that Christian workers can celebrate their holiday.

4. Jews by Choice, interfaith families, and their extended families confront special December dilemmas. Potential conflicts and misunderstandings can be averted by anticipating and discussing these issues in advance—by talking with one another, consulting a rabbi or other clergyman, reading books addressed to families with these issues, and participating in workshops offered by Jewish Family Services and synagogues.

Gifts of Love

Hanukkah is almost here and Rachel has a dilemma. She cannot find the family menorah, which disappeared after her mother's death 18 months ago. Sad and withdrawn since their loss, unable to enjoy the holidays, Rachel's father is unapproachable on the subject. Rachel determines to make a family celebration, exhausting her savings to buy dreidls, candles, and small gifts for her brother and father. But she cannot afford a new menorah. With regret, she decides at least to make latkes for the family as a link to happy memories of the years when her mother was still alive.

In this contemporary children's story, *The Odd Potato*, Eileen Bluestone Sherman explores the meaning of family gift-giving. As Rachel finds a way to open communication about gifts in her family, other families can use Hanukkah as a time to look at their own ways of giving throughout the year.

For Americans, the influence of the society around us and its commercialism is undeniable. Our homes are flooded with mail-order catalogues and invaded by televised advertisements urging us to get the latest products. In *The Art of Jewish Living: Hanukkah*, Dr. Ron Wolfson points out that the traditional time for *mishloach manot* (exchanging gifts) in the Jewish calendar is actually Purim, but because of "the influence of Christmas and its commercialization, gift-giving has become a major part of the modern Hanukkah celebration." Dr. Wolfson, who directs the Shirley and Arthur Whizin Center and Institute for Jewish Family Life at the University of

Judaism in Los Angeles, emphasizes that "one's approach to the buying, giving and receiving of gifts reflects important values."

For families hit by economic hardship, the extreme pressure to spend money they don't have at this time of year can be very painful. Louis Jacobs, LCSW, executive director of the Jewish Big Brother/Big Sister League, notes that his agency is seeing "many more families who are economically hard-pressed and feeling terrible about not being able to give to their children." The League serves many single-parent families where the father is absent and either marginally involved or completely uninvolved. These families have real needs for daily necessities like clothing. Jacobs' agency tries to help mothers avoid the seasonal buying mentality and find creative, economical solutions to gift-giving.

Even families that are intact are also feeling the financial effects of salary freezes or job loss. Children are aware of less money for clothes, eating out, and vacations. This hardship may be even more evident at holiday time, but parents need not automatically feel guilty about what they cannot provide. They should not assume that their children perceive this as a hardship. Parents should focus instead on what they *can* give.

It is natural for parents to want to give gifts to their children as an expression of their love, to want the best for their children. It is also natural for children to expect gifts at certain occasions. Peer pressure, which becomes important around the fourth grade and intensifies in adolescence, influences these expectations. Parents can acknowledge and satisfy their child's need to belong, to be accepted by peers, without buying every "in" product their child requests and without feeling controlled by their child.

Many parents try to satisfy their own needs by giving gifts to their children. A father feeling guilty for not spending enough time with his son buys him an expensive computer game to compensate. A mother who never had money for frills tries to make up for her own loss by getting her daughter costly jewelry. A divorced parent courts his children's loyalty by presenting them with designer clothes and taking an expensive trip, knowing the other parent cannot afford these luxuries.

These feelings of loss, guilt and desire for approval are normal in adults. However, it is important for parents to make a conscious attempt to separate their *own* needs from those of their child, and to focus on their *child's* needs.

What kinds of gifts do children want? Children were asked in an informal survey, "What is the best gift you have received from your parents?" The answers ranged from computer games and table hockey to a doll that had belonged to a little girl's grandmother and "my trip to Israel last summer." One six-year-old said, "I have so many toys, I don't know who gave me what. What I like best is a kiss and a hug from Mom and Dad." A thirteen-year-old had this advice: "It shouldn't be something the person thinks the child should have. It should be something really special to the person getting the gift. *Ask the child* what she wants."

What children want, then, are gifts that are chosen with care, that recognize their individuality, and that have a special meaning to them. The anticipation and excitement are part of their enjoyment. A gift that lasts is more valued. These kinds of gifts do not have to be costly. "Books are the most marvelous gifts you can give," says Lou Jacobs, who recommends inscribing them. His mother has a family tradition of stocking children's books. Each time the grandchildren visit, they can choose a book to take home. Another grandparent frequents garage and used book sales, selecting children's books to send to his grandchildren. "They don't care that the books were used, and they love getting the surprise packages," he comments. Other gifts particularly appropriate for Hanukkah, suggested by Ron Wolfson, are Jewish records and tapes, Hanukkah gelt commemorative coins from the Bank of Israel, and a *hanukkiyah* (Hanukkah menorah) for each child which will become a family heirloom.

In choosing gifts for their children, it is up to parents to state their values and set limits. If possible, let children help choose their gifts from a range of acceptable choices that you provide. Avoiding extreme rigidity lessens the potential for rebellion. For example, if you don't approve of the violence in a popular toy or movie, but your child is dying to be part of the craze, get something relatively harmless and inexpensive, such as a T-shirt or hat. In addition, what adults *do* often speaks louder than what they *say* about their values.

If status cars and clothes don't matter to parents, their children may be less attracted to expensive fads.

Make children aware that you have a family budget. Be frank about your financial circumstances, at a level each child can understand without being frightened. If what your older child wants exceeds what you can afford, offer to pay part and let the child earn the money for the rest. On Hanukkah, give your children choices: several small gifts or one expensive gift, for example.

In divorced families, gift-giving is one way each parent communicates his or her values, according to Joan Kristall, LCSW-C, director of Jewish Family Services Programs for Families of Separation, Divorce and Remarriage. If the parents cannot agree, it is not helpful to give negative messages about what the other is doing, nor can one parent control the behavior of the other. It is best for parents to follow their own values and give their children a sense of their financial realities, hoping that the children will sort out their own values as they mature.

Parents can shape their children's attitudes about gifts from an early age. This is the time to teach children the joys of giving. Youngsters love to make cards and gifts for their parents. How many Bubbies still proudly display the clay sculpture or first drawing their child, now an adult, made so many years ago? From this children can learn that putting time and oneself into a gift enhances its value to the recipient. When buying a gift, parents can help a child choose something appropriate to the recipient, such as gardening tools for a grandparent who loves planting. The good feelings between giver and receiver are not necessarily associated with a price tag, but with a loving relationship.

Ron Wolfson writes of a family that designates one night of Hanukkah as the "Gift of Self Night," exchanging non-monetary gifts only; another night is "Giving Night" when everyone gives to a charity of his or her choice. Parents model sharing our blessings with those in need by giving *tzedakah* on holidays.

Children can sometimes be their parents' teachers. In *The Odd Potato*, Rachel's father plans to fly his children to visit their cousins as a Hanukkah surprise. What Rachel really wants, however, is a celebration in their own home that will bring the family closer together after the loss of her mother. By turning the grocer's last potato into a menorah, as her mother had described her own destitute grandparents doing in Europe, Rachel helps her father find the most special Hanukkah gift, the lost family menorah. The candles, songs, games, and gathering of family and friends at Hanukkah—these are what children remember. The glow can continue all year round.

Suggestions for Meaningful Gift Giving

1. Give children gifts from the heart, remembering that the most expensive are not necessarily what children need or will value the most. Give creatively.

2. Avoid giving with negative messages like "Look at all I've done for you" or "I really can't afford this, but I'm buying it for you, anyway."

3. Give gifts that will last, acquiring deeper meaning over time, and that are appropriate for the individual recipient and the occasion.

4. Be honest with your children about the realities of your family, particularly your values and budget.

5. Blend giving with receiving; share a happy occasion with others through *tzedakah*. At this season, many schools and synagogues collect food, clothing and toys for the needy. Let your children help select items to contribute.

So Many Hamans ...
Helping Young Children Respond to Anti-Semitism

It's 9:00 a.m. on the Sunday before Purim. A mother and son are having a delightful, sticky time making hamentaschen. Suddenly their happy mood is shattered by a radio broadcast. A bus has been blown up by Hamas terrorists in Jerusalem. At least nineteen Jews are dead in the third attack in a single week.

Tears of anguish and anger fall on the hamentaschen. In an instant, the questions and messages of Purim have come to life. "Why do they want to stamp out the Jews?" asks the child. Why has it repeatedly been so during our history? The Talmud says, "When [the Hebrew month of] Adar arrives, we increase our joy" because Purim is coming (Ta'anit 29a). But how can we celebrate our survival as a people with total joy when we are still under attack? Driving home this question, a fourth bombing, this time in Tel Aviv, occurs the very next day.[1]

"So many Hamans, but just one Purim," goes a Yiddish proverb. Does this mean that our sense of vulnerability and persecution weighs as the heaviest element of our Jewish identity? Is this a message we want to give our children? How does the awareness of anti-

---

[1] In February and March 1996, a succession of four suicide bombings in Israel killed 60 people in nine days. The deadly attacks took place in Jerusalem, Ashkelon, and Tel Aviv.

Semitism affect a young child's sense of security and positive identification with the Jewish people?

Hatred of Jews is a reality which we can't hide from children. We are affected by terrorist attacks on our fellow Jews in Israel or anywhere in the world. Even elementary school age children hear about these events on the news, listen to adults discussing them, and observe their parents' reactions. In addition, they are beginning to learn about the Holocaust and other tragic chapters of Jewish history in Hebrew school.

What happens when children are directly and personally touched by anti-Semitism? Although American Jewry today is more secure than Diaspora Jewry has ever been, the Anti-Defamation League still logged 1,843 anti-Semitic incidents in this country in 1995. We have been spared the kind of brutal terrorism to which Israelis are subjected. Instead, anti-Semitism in America takes the forms of harassment, threats, and assaults; anti-Jewish and anti-Zionist writing and rhetoric; and vandalism of Jewish institutions.

A young child may first experience anti-Semitism by seeing her synagogue defaced by a faceless perpetrator. Or she may hear an adult make a derogatory remark about Jews. Perhaps it's a teacher who says, "What? You're missing another day of school for one of those Jewish holidays?" Some children encounter teasing or taunts from other children in the neighborhood or at school.

"The idea that people hate you just because you're Jewish is a scary thing for little children," says Marsha Tishler, coordinator of Holocaust Programs for the Baltimore Jewish Council. Haman's genocidal plot against the Jews of Persia was hatched in response to Mordechai's refusal to bow down to a human. "It is discomfiting to be singled out for being different—for any reason. . . . For young children who are still struggling to feel secure in the world of others, persecution is an evil that is truly terrifying," writes Rabbi Steven M. Rosman, co-author, with Kerry M. Olitzky and David P. Kasakove, of *When Your Jewish Child Asks Why.*

How should parents respond? Young children cannot understand the complex historical, economic, sociological, and religious reasons for hatred of the Jews. The most important things parents can do, according to Rabbi Rosman, are to help their children "feel safe and secure . . . and to maintain their children's self-respect and their respect for other people."

Some guidelines for helping a child deal with an anti-Semitic incident are presented at the end of this chapter.

The hamentaschen we eat on Purim can become a vehicle for putting anti-Semitism in perspective for children. These pastries are filled with meaning as well as with prunes or poppyseeds. In a hamentasch, the evil Haman (and all his subsequent embodiments) co-exist with the playfulness of Purim and the joy of our people's survival.

Young children think concretely. Through their senses, they can grasp the significance of the many other Jewish symbols that contain contradictory elements, reflecting the complexity of life. The gaiety of Purim is preceded by the sobriety of the Fast of Esther. The charoset eaten at the Passover Seder reminds us of the harshness of slavery yet the sweetness of freedom. We break a glass at the end of a wedding to show that happiness is not unadulterated. Sadness and joy are intermingled. But, as the hamentash and the charoset taste good, so Judaism should be appealing to children.

Our goals are to build self-esteem and strong, positive Jewish identity in young children. "Our Jewish identity is not defined by external persecution," says Rita Plaut, Judaic studies teacher in the Middle School at Krieger Schechter Day School. We do not want to make children fearful. "Let them first get a positive sense of self and of belonging to their immediate community," advises Marsha Tishler of the Baltimore Jewish Council.

"So many Hamans, but just one Purim." Although we have not been able to blot out anti-Semitism, Rabbi Steven Rosman says, "Still, we can strive to make our children feel protected when they are threatened, loved when they encounter hatred, and proud of their Jewish heritage when they face anti-Semitism."

Helping Children Deal with Anti-Semitism

1. Don't over-react or react *for* your child.
2. Ask questions to clarify what happened.
3. Find out how your child feels about what took place, and what he thinks about why it happened.

4. Reassure your child. Make him feel protected.

5. Affirm your child's self-worth.

6. Keep communication open. Your child may need to work through the experience by discussing it again.

7. Emphasize the positives. Painful situations in life can help us grow. Ask, "Would you do something differently next time?"

8. Many anti-Semitic remarks and acts are based on myths, stereotypes, and lack of accurate information or understanding. Is there an opportunity here for educating a teacher or a playmate?

9. Instead of labelling "bad (or good) people," talk about "people who do or say bad (or good) things."

10. As early as preschool, begin talking with your child about differences among people. Discuss and model the need to respect and learn about those who are different from us.

11. Set an example of taking action to combat anti-Semitism by writing a letter to a newspaper, attending a community rally, speaking to your child's school administration or his class.

12. To counter the image of the Jew as victim, point out historical and contemporary examples of Jewish strength and triumph over adversity and oppression.

13. Turn to local community resources for help: rabbis, Hebrew and day school teachers, the Anti-Defamation League, Jewish Family Services, and Jewish libraries and resource centers, where staff can help you select age-appropriate books and tapes.

Passover: Opening the Door to Children's Questions

"Ma nishtanah . . . ?" Why is this night different from all other nights? Virtually every Jew can remember, as a child, saying the Four Questions at the Passover Seder. For a few minutes, the youngest one—sometimes nervous, sometimes self-assured—is at center stage, the focus of *everyone*'s attention. Usually, the child is vigorously applauded after the recitation.

The Passover Seder is the single most observed Jewish practice in the United States today. More Jewish households keep this tradition than any other, including lighting Shabbat or Chanukah candles and contributing to Jewish charities, according to the Council of Jewish Federations' 1990 National Jewish Population Survey. Thus, for many Jews, the Seder is their *only* connection to Judaism. Because it takes place in the home, with several generations present, the Seder offers a perfect opportunity for enhancing communication between parents and children, and a rich source of wisdom to draw on through the years.

What we can teach children through the Seder is the importance of asking questions. From the Four Questions, the whole Seder unfolds. The child's role is essential. The goal of the service is to get children to ask: "Why do we celebrate this holiday? What is this all about?" Questions are very important in Judaism because they are a way of learning, says Rena Rotenberg, MA, Director of Early Childhood Education at the Council on Jewish Education Services. The

Talmud and rabbinic commentaries on the Torah, with their endless and intricate questions, answers, and debates, are all posited on the premise that asking leads to deeper understanding.

There are many kinds of questions and many ways of asking. The Passover Haggadah provides a ready-made framework for helping parents to understand how their children ask questions and how to answer them, in the section describing the four sons: one who is wise, one who is wicked (or rebellious), one who is simple, and one who does not know how to ask. These four children represent a range of personalities, learning styles, and levels of maturity. Commenting on this passage in the Rabbinical Assembly's *Passover Haggadah: The Feast of Freedom*, editor Rachel Anne Rabinowicz says, "The rabbis counseled that the story of the Exodus should be geared to the attitude and age of the questioner." Based on the Talmudic commentary, we can expand this to a general principle for parents: "The parent should teach each child on the level of the child's understanding." (*Pesahim* 116a.)

The passage about the four children can be viewed "either as a description of four different children, or as a description of the same child going through developmental stages," say Rabbi Judith Z. Abrams and Dr. Steven A. Abrams in *Jewish Parenting: Rabbinic Insights.* Most children will probably go through the four phases: the very young child who does not know enough to ask, the child who knows enough to ask simple questions, the rebellious child separating from his parents and rejecting tradition, and the child who has attained the intellectual and emotional maturity to be interested in the subject for himself. Another way to look at this process is that children ask different kinds of questions at different ages, and the same question may be answered differently, in more depth, as the child matures.

Here are some insights into different kinds of questioners, and advice for parents on how to respond.

The simple child: Young children think very concretely, asking about what they see, says early childhood educator Rena Rotenberg. Lacking a wide vocabulary, they may understand more than they can say. To find out what the child is really asking, the parent can rephrase the question in the form of a statement, reflecting it back to the child. (Dina: "Why did you put salt in that bowl of water?" Mom: "I see you noticed I put a bowl of water on the table and I put salt in it." Dina: "Yes, I want to know what it's for." Mom: "Have you ever tasted your tears when you cry?") Acknowledge the child from where he is. Break up the subject into little, understandable pieces, and repeat explanations if necessary.

The child who does not know how to ask: Some parents worry because their child *doesn't* ask questions or communicate easily. The Haggadah advises these parents: "You should open the discussion for him." This child is part of the family and must be included—but how? Rena Rotenberg suggests an indirect approach to get a child to talk, such as reading a book and then using it as a jumping off point for a discussion. Conducting a conversation or listening while busying oneself at another task, such as preparing dinner, without looking directly at the child, may free him from feelings of being scrutinized and enable him to ask. Perhaps this is why so many children bring up questions that take parents by surprise while driving in the car. Parents also need to wonder, "Why is my child not asking?" Perhaps the child feels the parent is not accessible. Or maybe the child's earlier questions were not answered with sensitivity ("What a silly question!" "You don't need to know that.")—and so the child simply stops asking.

The child who asks constantly: Though not one of the four sons in the Haggadah, this is a child many parents describe as driving them to distraction with questions. Non-stop whys are developmentally typical of three-year-olds, who are trying to make sense of a world in which so much is new. But they can add to the stress of the parent who is preoccupied with a hundred other concerns. First, try to find out why the child is asking that question at that time. Does he want information, or is he dealing with some fear and asking for reassurance? Perhaps he is simply trying to get your undivided attention. You may need to tell him, "I can't answer you right now, but we will talk about it right after dinner"—and do it. It helps to leave a little time after work for both parent and child to make the transition to home. Creating some regular special time for you and your child alone also goes a long way.

The rebellious child: Asking provocative questions and "removing

oneself from the community," as the Haggadah puts it, is appropriate behavior for adolescents, whose task is to work out their own
identity. Some younger children may also respond in this way. Consider whether the child is behaving perversely because adults in the
past have responded to his questions by mocking or demeaning.
Keep in mind that if he is asking, he is already involved. Children
absorb information in different ways. For this child, as for the one
who does not ask, indirect ways to draw him in sometimes are most
effective. Approach the subject through the child's own interests.
Allow her to participate in a hands-on way. (For example, in the
context of Passover, this child could help set the table, prepare the
food, make place cards, or dress up in a costume.) Finally, you can
talk about a subject with someone else, in the child's presence; or
make it part of your family dinner conversation.

Rabbi and Dr. Abrams comment that "By inculcating in our children a sense of self-esteem and a love of Judaism in the first two
phases of life . . . we may 'inoculate' them, as it were, against doing
the most self-destructive things in adolescence. And no matter how
pugnacious they may become, we still include them."

The wise child: This child is motivated and eager to learn, says
Rabbi Stuart Seltzer, Director of the Rosenbloom Religious School
at Chizuk Amuno Congregation. Because the wise child has a good
background of knowledge, he or she can pose specific, well-formed
questions. What a joy it is for a parent to engage in dialogue with a
child who genuinely wants to learn. The parent's role is to foster this
love of learning in every way possible.

The Seder presents the role of parents as encouraging children to
ask questions. What to do, however, with questions that parents are
not comfortable answering? Some parents feel that certain topics are
"off limits." Your response may depend on your child's age. With the
younger child, find out what she's really asking, advises Rena Rotenberg. A children's book, or even a picture, can help both parents and
child talk about challenging subjects, such as sexuality, divorce,
God, or death. With an older child, you might say, "I'm not really
comfortable talking about this, but let's try to find someone who is."

What the Seder teaches us is that growth and learning come
about when we pose questions. The *process* is more important than

the result. Commentary in The Rabbinical Assembly Haggadah stresses the message that "the simplest question can have many answers . . . as life itself is fraught with complexity and contradictions. . . . To accept the fact that not every problem can be neatly resolved is another stage of liberation. . . . Acknowledging that some things are beyond our understanding is a sign of faith." Parents do not need to feel that they must have definitive answers to every question their child asks.

This year, try using the Seder as a workshop to open the doors to communication. Invite everyone present to ask questions and suggest answers. Experience the excitement of one question leading to another. Turn to the youngest child and say, "Look what you started by asking four little questions!" Hearing their parents ask questions conveys a beautiful lesson to children: that inquiry and learning are parts of a lifelong process, one that families can enjoy together.

Fielding Questions

1. When deciding how to answer children's questions, consider their age, developmental level, individual personality, learning style, and relationship with you.

2. Be open to your child's questioning. Listen, and try to determine what he or she really wants to know at that time.

3. It's O.K. to let your child know you need some time to think about your answer, but do respond within a reasonable amount of time. Remember that younger children lose interest sooner than and can't wait as long as older ones.

4. Model asking questions yourself, as one of the best paths to learning throughout life.

Making the Most of Summer

Jarad is angry at his parents. After working hard in school all year, he has been looking forward to the freedom summer will afford him. What he wants is to stay home, hang around with the neighborhood kids, swim at the local pool, and spend a week at the beach with his family. But Mom and Dad have just blown away Jarad's dreams. As full-time working parents, Susan and Bill cannot allow Jarad, at age ten, to stay home without proper supervision. On top of that, they inform their son that, due to Bill's frozen salary, a week at the beach in peak season is out of the question this year. "We're sorry," Susan and Bill tell Jarad, sad that they cannot meet their son's expectations.

Parents, too, approach summer with expectations of more time to relax and to enjoy being together as a family. But that doesn't always happen. Responsibilities and pressures continue; the weather is too hot or too rainy; and the kids are bored and bickering.

Although the weather is out of our control, many disappointments that arise during the summer can be avoided with advance planning. Call a family meeting, giving each parent and child a chance to express a wish list for the summer. Then look at the realities, considering such factors as time, budget, responsibilities, and needs of each person. Allow your children to voice their feelings. Listen, and acknowledge them, especially if you cannot satisfy all their wishes. Then come up with a family plan that finds a balance between expectations and realities.

"In retrospect," Susan says, "if we had given Jarad a chance earlier to tell us his desires for the summer, we could have lessened his frustration. The best resolution we could find was to enroll Jarad in a day camp run by the Department of Recreation for most of the summer. We're planning a weekend instead of a week at the beach. In addition, Bill and I will take a few days for the whole family to stay home, relax, and go on day trips together."

Each family has its own particular circumstances to consider in planning. When older children go away to camp for at least part of the summer, other arrangements are needed for the time they are at home. For many families, the summer remains as tightly scheduled as the rest of the year, with parents continuing to work, and the children in day care, day camp, or other structured programs. The family's normal patterns of operation are disrupted, however, because the children now have a *different* routine. This can be especially stressful for single parents.

Another scenario occurs when a working parent has the summer off or when a parent does not work away from home. In these households, both children and parent now find themselves with the luxury of daily leisure and no set routine. This situation can become either a burden or an opportunity.

Whatever pattern fits your family, your child may need help making the transition from a scheduled program during the academic year to a diminished—or a different—structure over the summer. In addition to a change in routine, many children also experience a loss of friends whom they may not see until September. Acclimating to a change of pace and circumstances takes time and effort. Try to build in a few unscheduled days for unwinding, both at the beginning and at the end of the summer.

How much structure does a child need? Each child is unique, and some children need more structure than others, even in the same family. In planning summer activities, consider a range of variables, such as your child's age and temperament. Does she like and need frequent contact with peers? Can he find ways to entertain himself for hours at a time? Does she enjoy quiet pursuits like reading and art, or does she like to be physically active? Children generally need a combination of free time for themselves and with the family, as well as some structured activities. Dr. Joan Bergstrom, professor of education at Wheelock College and author of *School's Out! Resources for Your Child's Time*, encourages parents to let children make some of these choices for themselves.

Changing our rhythm during the summer has many benefits. "I welcome the longer summer days because there's more time to read with my son, tend the garden together, or even lie on our backs and cloud gaze," says Barbara, a teacher and mother of a four-year-old. David, an accountant in a downtown firm, takes advantage of Shabbat coming later in the summer. "By continuing to leave work early now, as I do in the winter, I get to spend extra time with my family, helping to prepare for Shabbat, playing with the children, or taking a walk to talk about how the day went," he says.

Seasonal change also provides an opportunity for self-discovery, a window for seeing and hearing things differently, allowing for change and growth. A beautiful prayer by the great Hasidic Rabbi Nachman of Bratzlav (1772–1811) expresses this "stretching" of the spirit:

> *Master of the Universe,*
> *Grant me the ability to be alone;*
> *May it be my custom to go outdoors each day*
> *among the trees and grasses,*
> *among all growing things*
> *and there may I be alone,*
> *and enter into prayer*
> *to talk with the One*
> *that I belong to.*

Many children today complain of boredom when left to their own devices. In this age of hyper-stimulation from video games, television, and packed schedules, one of the greatest gifts parents can give a child is the ability to develop her own inner resources and learn how to enjoy her own company. The more relaxed pace of summer offers many such opportunities.

A mother may find that her child, who tends to move slowly, has an easier time hearing her during the summer when she is not rushing him to get out in the morning. As mother and son find they both enjoy the slower pace, they may look for ways to approach their schedule differently in the fall so as to reduce stress and make more special time for themselves, alone and together.

Parents may want to adjust the usual family rules to meet the special needs of summer. Perhaps bedtimes and curfews can be extended. On July 4th, one parent bundled his children, who had already been put to bed, into the car in their pajamas to go see some fireworks that were unexpectedly visible in a nearby park. It can be refeshing for children to see their parents relax, do something spontaneous, and have fun, too.

Evaluating your family's needs and planning ahead for the summer build communication, trust and respect among parents and children. Taking this approach to summer plans can also improve your family's skills at averting collisions between expectations and realities that arise all year round.

Suggestions for Family Summer Planning

1. When children are home all summer, plan a mixture of structured and unstructured activities, perhaps in alternating weeks. Take advantage of free public activities such as concerts and park programs.

2. Use summer as an opportunity to allow your child to try something new without having to make a large commitment of time or money. Try a week of drama or nature camp, an art program for grandparents and grandchildren at a museum, or a different sport.

3. While Hebrew school is out, use some summer leisure time to continue your child's Jewish education in a way that will be fun. Read books of Jewish interest, listen to Jewish music, explore Jewish sites on the Internet, and visit area Jewish museums together.

4. Create new summer family rituals such as sleeping out in the back yard or hosting a family reunion with a picnic. Not only does this help children see their parents in a new light, but it also rekindles pleasant childhood memories for parents.

Surviving Summer Camp

Mom and Dad,

Why did you send me to this place? I hate it here! No one is friendly to me. All the girls from last year know each other already. Our cabin smells and the food is horrible. I miss my own bed. PLEASE come and get me right away! I promise I'll do all my chores without being reminded, if you will *just take me home*.

Amy

Dear Mommy and Daddy,

I am having a ball at camp! Laura, the girl who sleeps in the bunk next to me, likes gymnastics and tennis, just like me. I passed my swimming test on the first day. On Friday night we had a beautiful Shabbat service outdoors under the trees. Dinners aren't as great as yours, but they're OK. I'm going to learn how to use a potter's wheel in arts and crafts. Why did you sign me up for only 4 weeks? Gotta run.

Love,
Sara

Children's responses to their summer camp experiences range over a broad spectrum, as these letters show. A child's first exposure to sleepaway camp can evoke much anxiety before departure and many problems once camp begins—or it can be a long-awaited and very positive adventure. Parents, too, are affected by and may share their children's feelings and reactions. But parents can also have a significant influence on how their children respond to camp. Children's experiences with camp are shaped by many variables, including previous life experiences, expectations, preparation, and the realities of the specific camp. How can parents help make their children's time away at camp most enjoyable and growth-enhancing?

For parents, the idea of sending children to camp brings up bittersweet feelings that are connected to issues of separation. On the one hand, the recognition that their children are growing up—becoming more independent, able to function on their own in a different setting, and learning to turn to other adults—can be quite positive for parents. In addition, parents may look forward to a little more free time to themselves and a little more space. Along with these hopeful and happy feelings, however, parents also feel sad because they realize that some of the special closeness of childhood between parent and child is being left behind. So while parents want this opportunity for their child, they have mixed feelings, which may be mirrored in the child.

Children's ability to handle the camp separation is related to their previous experiences in dealing with separation. A child who has a history of medical difficulties, separation or divorce of parents, or loss of a significant person or pet may have a harder time, as going to camp will stir up memories of previous separations. Parents might think back to their own experiences of separating in life and the ambivalent feelings they had. "What helped me through the hard times as a new camper," says Joan, age 32, "was making new friends, turning to camp counselors, and staying in contact with the people back home important to me." Adults can recall feeling proud when they mastered dealing with a separation, taking real delight in a new experience.

In planning for camp for their children, parents should be aware of the kinds of difficulties children might experience. These range from feeling homesick, being placed in a bunk different from that of a friend, feeling teased by other children, or not getting along with a counselor, to not liking various aspects of daily living such as the food, certain activities, and being required to make their bed each day, keep their bunk clean, or go on an overnight hike.

Sometimes parents will recognize that their children's difficulties at camp are similar to ones they have at home. For example, the child who has trouble getting along with other children at home may wish that relationships at camp would go more smoothly. When there is a fresh start, this is possible. More often, though, patterns that happen at home are replayed at camp.

Children also find it difficult when they know something unusual is going on at home. Andy, age 9, wondered if his new baby sister was getting all the attention in his absence. Other children may worry if a grandparent is ill or if their parents have recently separated.

How can parents best anticipate these difficulties and prepare their child for camp? Ed Cohen, Executive Director of Camps Airy and Louise in Thurmont and Cascade, Maryland, observes that a number of children come to camp carrying their parents' anxieties based on problems the parents encountered when they were campers. Telling your child, "Try it one day; if you don't like it, I'll come and get you" gives the camp staff nothing positive with which to work, Cohen says.

Some parents send their children to camp feeling they can't handle parental responsibilities all summer, whether it is because of job commitments or for other reasons. It is important to communicate with children about *why* they are going to camp, especially for those who are uncertain about wanting to go, without giving them a message of rejection. Illene Poall, Assistant Director of Camp Pinemere in Stroudsburg, Pennsylvania, advises parents to present camp to their children as a chance to have a multitude of experiences they would not ordinarily have—opportunities to try new activities, participate in the camp spirit, make new friends, have fun, and grow up in some ways.

Summer camps can also provide important opportunities for experiences that will enhance the child's Jewish identity and commitment. Through Shabbat programs, cultural events and Torah study, campers discover new ways to enjoy their Jewish heritage during the summer. Jewish camps, affiliated with every denomination and Jewish youth group, can add a new dimension to the spiritual lives of the campers and create a positive connection to Judaism for years to come.

It is also important, though, to let children know that it may be hard, that there may be times when they will feel homesick or left out or discouraged. Ed Cohen suggests making children aware that "each child is not in the spotlight all the time, but one of a group of 12 or 13 who must share the spotlight, unlike what occurs in most homes." Tell your child that the counselors at camp will be there to help with these feelings and that other children will also be dealing with similar issues.

Another way of preparing is to give the camp essential information in advance, when appropriate. All parents seek a balance between giving their child an opportunity for a fresh start and giving the staff information that they might need to help the child. For example, if there has been a recent divorce or separation in the family, it is important to let the camp director know this ahead of time. If the child has a history of hyperactivity, is generally on medication, and has difficulty concentrating and following directions, let the director know what has worked at home, because sometimes those techniques can be helpful at camp. Mike Schneider, Director of Camp Airy in Thurmond, Maryland, says that informing camp personnel of any circumstances or health concerns that could influence a child's experience does not have to "set up a self-fulfilling prophecy; it is just important to make the camp aware." Select a camp where you can trust the director and staff to use this material sensitively and appropriately. Most camps welcome parents' help and want to work with them to make the child's experience successful.

Assure your child that you will be keeping him informed about things at home. You do not have to share every detail of a difficult situation, but a child who knows that someone is ill or that his parents are separating needs to be kept up-to-date about what is happening. If the child can maintain trust in you, he will be better able to put these matters aside and get into the rhythm at camp.

But what if—in spite of careful preparation—problems arise at camp? What if you are the parent who receives the letter from an angry, upset child? At first, you will feel worried. But then, step back and think, "Does my child generally cope well? Is it possible that Amy wrote about her homesick feelings during rest hour or nighttime when those feelings are more likely to occur? Are other aspects of camp going fairly well?" Of course, you can't know the answer, but think about whether you want to give the camp some time to work it out.

On the other hand, if the letter is really upsetting, it's important for the camp to know that your child has written this to you. In such a case, call the camp and ask the administrator to look into this situation and to contact you with a more detailed report of how your child is doing, what parts are going well, what parts are hard. Sometimes a child never even tells the counselor that she is unhappy. If the counselor knew, he or she could reach out more to the child.

The first week of camp last summer, Daniel's parents received a postcard that read, "Everybody's being mean to me; nobody likes me." "We were very concerned because Daniel usually gets along with his peers," says Daniel's father. "We called the director, who spoke with Daniel's counselor. It seems that Daniel's feelings of rejection were related to the kind of flare-up that occurs when children in the neighborhood very quickly gang up on another child and just as quickly make up, move on and become friends again. The incident assumed more significance in Daniel's mind because he was in a new, unfamiliar setting. A week later, he had made a couple of friends and had adjusted well. But speaking to the director reassured us."

What happens, however, if a child does leave camp early because of serious behavior difficulties or homesickness? Ed Cohen says many parents blame the camp and the child ("Look what you did to me"), presenting the situation as "win-or-lose." Cohen suggests parents look for the positives, view the experience as one of growth, and recognize the successes the child did achieve.

Staying in touch is crucial to making a child's experience at camp a good one. The most important means is mail. Ten-year-old Jennifer says, "Parents should know all kids love to get mail at camp. Parents should write *often*, even if they're short letters." Mike Schneider concurs: "Mail call is an extremely important part of the camp day. The disappointment of not receiving a letter when others are getting lots is at times overwhelming."

When you write to your child, be newsy, sharing what's happening at home. Give the child the message that you are handling your issues as the parent. It's important to convey to your child that even though he is no longer at home, you're still thinking of him, you're still present in his life. When you talk about missing him, try doing it on a light note: "The dinner table tonight was so quiet without your usual jokes," or "Your brother misses you. He doesn't like having to feed the dog every single day." Illene Poall suggests that working parents stress in their letters that the normal, daily routine is continuing at home, and they are glad their child is in a place with so many more opportunities for fun and excitement. "Parents who are not working might note how few children are in town and how quiet the pool is, whereas camp is like having a sleepover party every night," she says.

Another way to stay in contact is by sending care packages, which children love to get. Camps have different policies; some allow parents to send food; others do not. It is important to remember to respect the camp's policy on *kashrut* whenever you send food to your child. Some camps permit treats, which can be simple, like balloons, joke books, or Hebrew games. If your care package contains items for your child to share with his bunkmates, it will be better received in the camp setting.

Camps also have different policies about visiting and telephone calls. Follow the specified guidelines. While conveying your willingness to listen to homesick feelings or worried questions, let your child know in a light way that you miss her, think about her and are eager to hear about camp activities.

Some parents view their child's time at camp as an opportunity for them to have a vacation on their own. Parents who do go away during this time should prepare their child, furnishing information about places where they can be reached or names of alternate people who can be called. This will reassure the child, who needs a sense of security about home in order to relax in the camp setting.

The keys to a successful camp experience for parent and child are preparation, encouragement, and communication. So start licking stamps and addressing envelopes now, and keep those letters coming!

Suggestions to Enhance Your Child's Camp Experience

1. Remove from your child's luggage your own anxieties based on your experience as a camper. Allow him to experience camp for himself.

2. Prepare your child with information about what to expect at camp. Present camp as an opportunity for new experiences and growth. In a camp with a Jewish program, this can mean a chance to participate in "joyous Jewish living"[1] in a communal setting.

3. Write to your child frequently.

4. Maintain good communication with the camp staff before and during the season.

---

[1]Rabbi Sheldon Dorph, Ed.D., "Camp Ramah," *Women's League Outlook*, Winter 1991, p. 16.

L'Dor Va-Dor

Focus on Fatherhood

Centuries ago, the authors of the Babylonian Talmud set down the job description of a father. "A father is obligated to circumcise his son, redeem him, teach him Torah, take a wife for him, and teach him a trade. Some authorities add, teach him to swim, also. What is the reason? His life may depend on it." (*Kiddushin*, 29a and 30b). "A father must provide for his daughter clothing and covering and must also give her a dowry so that people may be anxious to woo her and so proceed to marry her." (*Ketubbot*, 52b)

Much has changed since these words were written in the sixth century. Daughters and sons in our time receive similar preparation for life. However, in its emphasis on the importance and nature of fathers' work in raising children, this ancient dictum resounds with meaning today.

Meet Alan, Ira, and Jeffrey, three fathers spanning several generations.[1] Alan, 75 and retired, has four adult children in their 30s and 40s scattered across the country. Ira, 48, is also the father of four, ranging in age from 10 to 18, with the oldest about to leave home. Jeff, at 30, has a one-year-old and a three-year-old.

Our three modern dads are also links in an ancient line of Jewish fathers extending back to Abraham, Isaac, and Jacob, whose influ-

---

[1]This chapter focuses on intact families with married parents. Although many of the aspects of parenting presented here apply to all fathers, families of divorce face unique issues which are addressed in other chapters.

ence we daily acknowledge in praising "our God and God of our fathers." Listening to these men's voices, we can reflect on what has changed about fathers' roles and what common threads bind the generations together.

Alan, Ira, and Jeff have a lot in common, in spite of their age differences. All made conscious decisions to be parents and want to play a significant part in their children's lives. Like most middle-class men of his generation, Alan worked while his wife stayed home with the children. However, while many of his contemporaries willingly accepted a clear division of labor between the father as breadwinner and the mother as caretaker, Alan regretted that his long working hours left him little time for the family. When his schedule improved, he loved to spend his free time with the children, building things for them, biking, sledding, getting up early to make pancakes, and going on family picnics.

Having experienced the Depression, Alan speaks more than the younger fathers about financial worries. Alan defines his chief responsibilities as providing for his family and planning for the future, especially his children's—and even his grandchildren's— education. Proud of his children's achievements, Alan nonetheless feels that a father's job is never done. A parable told by the Hasidic rabbi of Radamsko in the 1800s expresses this view. "A passenger on a ship impatiently awaited the day when it would reach port. When the ship neared the harbor, a storm drove it back to sea, much to the dismay of the traveler." Even in adulthood, children's problems trouble their parents' rest. "Parents should help out in time of need," says Alan. "I continue to worry about my kids; it's hard to let go."

Still near the beginning of his voyage as a father of very young children, Jeff says the only problems so far have been loss of sleep and of flexibility in his schedule, necessitating the sacrifice of some personal time and pursuits. As Erik Erikson observed in *Childhood and Society*, "A baby's presence exerts a persistent domination over the outer and inner lives of every member of the household. Because these members must reorient themselves to accommodate his presence, they must also grow as individuals and as a group." Jeff savors each developmental milestone, loves playing with his children, and delights in their special time together. "Of all the things I've done in my life, being a father is definitely the best," he confides.

Ira wistfully looks back on those simpler "good old days" from the throes of his children's adolescence. What makes this stage so difficult, he says, is that "in searching for their identity, adolescents rebel against the things that are most important to you. Also, you have less control as a parent. It hurts when your child doesn't communicate or no longer wants to do things with the family." His advice to other parents? "Keep telling your kids that you are always there for them. Give them good values in their early years, keep feeding them the values, and hope they take hold."

All of the fathers stressed the importance of defining one's values and teaching them to children. Those highlighted by Alan include self-reliance, safety, Jewish identity, education, respect for the earth, social service, and developing multiple interests—a list strikingly similar to the Talmudic instructions about what fathers should teach children.

A related theme important to these fathers is respecting the individuality of each child. They emphasize listening to and valuing their children's opinions, encouraging them to question, giving them choices and allowing them to make decisions.

Respect for each child cuts across gender lines. Alan taught his sons and daughters alike to work with tools, engage in sports, cook, and develop marketable skills. "I could see the economy was changing," he says, "and I didn't expect the girls would stay home with their children as my wife had." It is important for fathers to get in touch with their attitudes about gender roles and to ask what expectations they are setting for their children in such areas as athletics, the arts, domestic tasks, choices of toys, attitudes toward work, and definitions of success.

The behavior that parents model for their children communicates strong messages. If Dad and Mom share household chores and child-rearing responsibilities, if they interact in supportive, caring ways, children view that as the norm. Fathers today still have many responsibilities to juggle, but they are making more of an attempt to participate in raising the children with their wives. Men are finding more satisfactions in parenting. They are also discovering that sharing the challenges and joys of parenting can strengthen their bonds with their mates. Says journalist Ari Goldman in an essay on "Jewish Fathering," "Men are learning to be fathers in new ways."

One area of change noted by modern fathers is an increased desire and ability to communicate with children, to express feelings and affection. Dr. Frank Pittman has described how men have been shut off from these modes of experience by "the masculine mystique," a set of attitudes defining masculinity in ways that can make our lives "limited, lonely, and painful." A survey of contemporary Father's Day cards reveals a recurring theme: "Father's Day is a time for sharing feelings that we don't talk about often enough." In one card, the responsibility for the child's lack of communication, sadly, is transferred to the father: "A dad is someone who hears the 'thanks' even when it's unspoken."

Dr. Pittman finds that "what men most want to talk about, when the atmosphere is safe, is their failure to get close to their fathers." Rabbi Seymour Rosenbloom agrees: "What happens to men in their lives is often linked to unfinished business with their fathers."[1] Although it may be painful, exploring one's relationship with one's own father, understanding the lacks and seeking out the strengths, can help define the kind of parent one wants to be.

Boys need models of mature men to define their own masculinity, and they need to learn a variety of ways to be a man. Girls also benefit from positive male role models, who influence the kinds of relationships they will later form with men. Dr. Mark S. Komrad observes in his psychiatric practice at Sheppard Pratt Hospital a greater openness to emotions among younger men. As Jeff says, "Expressing feelings, hugging, and communicating are not unmanly; they are healthy."

Fathers as providers, planners, teachers, nurturers—the roles are complex and demanding. Our ancestors Abraham, Isaac and Jacob wrestled with the challenges of parenting, made mistakes, and experienced times of joy as we do today. Ari Goldman sees the Talmudic

---

[1]Quoted in Paul Benson, "Men: Going Through the Change," *Baltimore Jewish Times*, Jan. 28, 1994, pp. 26–27.

instruction of teaching a child to swim as "a blueprint for the modern father . . . who must teach his child to adapt to the ever-changing world, as a swimmer adapts to currents and waves." At the same time, fathers are being changed by their children and by the world around them. In this process of growth, our tradition still offers us values that can help keep a family on course.

Defining Dad: Suggestions for Fathers

1. In defining the kind of father you want to be, look at your own role models. Ask what you would like to emulate and what you would like to do differently.

2. Counseling and parent support groups can offer help in dealing with the challenges of being a father, including issues of communication with spouse and children.

3. While every couple works out its own division of labor, try to avoid creating a split between the "fun" parent and the "mean" disciplinarian.

4. Find opportunities for your children to see you playing a variety of roles, from work and home responsibilities to community service and recreation.

5. Build bonds with your children through shared family experiences, such as observing Jewish holidays, camping, sports, and reading together.

Holding on and Letting Go: How to Build a Healthy Relationship with Your Adult Child

Amy, a sophomore at a university in Boston, calls her parents in New Jersey daily. Steve phones home every Sunday from his Pennsylvania campus. Alex, a college freshman in Baltimore, and his mother Ellen, living in New York, call each other sporadically, whenever the spirit moves them.

These different rhythms of communication reflect a range of philosophies and styles of parents' involvement in the lives of their young adult children. As children leave home to start college, live on their own, or marry, their relationships with their parents frequently change. This period of transition, from age 18 into the early twenties, can unfold more smoothly if parents and children prepare by thinking about and discussing what they expect of each other and how they relate to each other. Each family, being unique, needs to find its own answers to these questions, but some pointers may be helpful.

The challenge most parents face as their children leave home is how to shift from the role of provider and protector to an adult-to-adult relationship. "All of us who have nurtured and taught children know . . . how deeply rooted is our love and need of our children," say Sharon Strassfeld and Kathy Green in *The Jewish Family Book*. "We do not want to lose our children. We watch them grow, and we see that as they move from one developmental stage to another, the nature of the parent-child relationship changes."

Parents are often ambivalent about this passage. Ellen says, "I feel relief that I've done my job, and all my children are now on their own. My husband and I finally have time for *us*. But we miss our kids, and sometimes I wonder if we did a good enough job raising them." Steve laughingly comments, "I'm a 25-year-old college graduate, with proven competence in my profession, but my Dad still reminds me to take my toothbrush when I go on a trip."

Young adult children may want to assert their independence, yet continue to feel the need for guidance and support from their parents at times. These mixed feelings in both parents and children are natural, and acknowledging them is a healthy first step to understanding how they affect family relationships.

Perhaps the hardest part of parenting grown children is accepting the loss of control. Young adults face many choices: friends, lifestyle, location, career, mate. With more options available and socially acceptable today than ever before, parents worry about the paths their children will take. Will Alex come home from first semester in college sporting a tattoo? What if he gets in with the "wrong" crowd? Will Amy choose the "right" major for a successful future? Will she use good judgment in her social relationships?

"Train a child in the way he ought to go, and even in old age, he will not swerve from it," says the Biblical book of Proverbs (22:6). "I wish I could be so certain that the upbringing we gave our children will guide them safely through life," reflects Barry, "but there are no guarantees. I know I need to be prepared for my children sometimes choosing to do things that feel uncomfortable to me."

Over the centuries, our rabbis debated this issue as they considered and adjudicated problems faced by ordinary people in their daily lives. Jewish laws about the limits of parental authority have focused on defining exactly what the child's responsibility to serve and revere his parents entails. One of the areas most frequently discussed was the child's choice of a mate. Gerald Blidstein explores various Biblical, Talmudic, medieval, and modern views of parent-child disagreements over marriage in *Honor Thy Father and Mother:*

Filial Responsibility in Jewish Law and Ethics. For example, in the sixteenth century, Rabbi Moses Isserles, one of the great halachic authorities in Poland, ruled that ". . . if the father objects to his son's marriage to the woman of his choice, the son is not obliged to listen to his father." (*Yore De'ah* 240:25) In all these discussions, it is clear that the issues are complex and require sensitivity to the basic principles on which the laws rest, as well as to the needs and wishes of both parent and child. Modern parents and adult children need sensitivity in communicating over areas of disagreement, as well.

Defining priorities and communicating them clearly to an adult child can help parents decide when to be flexible and when to take a firm stand. Some parents can accept their child's choice of what the parents consider unorthodox appearance or friends, but not the forsaking of family moral and religious values. Many draw the line at situations in which they fear their child's safety is at risk, such as travelling abroad in areas of unrest, driving in bad weather, or abusing alcohol or drugs.

When worry becomes an emotional burden, calm analysis helps. If you know your adult child does not drink and drive, or if she is with a group of friends who are responsible, look at the anxiety as *your* problem. To say, "I'll worry the whole two weeks you are travelling in Europe" puts the burden unfairly on your child.

Over-protecting a child prevents him from taking risks, making mistakes, and learning from them—a process essential for the development of self-esteem and confidence. The child gets the message that he is not able to take care of himself. Rabbi Shlomo Riskin, commenting on the Torah story of Joseph and his brothers, points out that if Joseph had stayed home, he would have smothered under the pressure of his father Jacob's love, unable to develop his own character and realize his destiny of becoming a leader.[1] Thinking back on her child-rearing years, Ellen says, "The risk of making our children feel inadequate to cope in the world seemed more damaging in the long run than their maybe getting hurt a few times."

How can parents establish an adult-to-adult relationship with

---

[1]Rabbi Shlomo Riskin, "Who's to Blame for Sibling Rivalry?," *Baltimore Jewish Times,* January 1, 1993.

their children? Mutual respect starts from birth, and being a good listener is very important, notes Barbara, a single parent whose daughter Sandy has returned home after graduating from college. Barbara and Ellen both began encouraging their children toward independence and decision-making in early childhood. They explained the reasons for family rules instead of simply imposing parental authority.

Adult children want to be accepted as the individuals they are by their parents. Yet young adults still want and appreciate their parents' praise and approval for their accomplishments.

As children mature, they realize that greater freedom entails more responsibility on their part. Some parents offer advice—whether requested or not—into adulthood. "When I ask for advice," says Sandy, "my Mom usually urges me to think through the situation and decide for myself." Parents need to be prepared for possible rejection of their advice even when their adult child has solicited it. It is best to avoid an "I told you so" reaction. Honesty may not always be the best policy if the child has made a decision that can't be changed, such as purchasing a home.

When an adult child chooses a direction that the parents simply cannot approve and that causes them pain, the parents need to pull back and recognize that their child must live his or her own life, and similarly, their lives must go on. If possible, they should try to affirm the areas in their relationship that they can share, and leave the door open to future communication.

Parents who relate to their adult children as adults find many positive elements in this new phase of their lives. Seeing one's children learn from their mistakes and use their education to make their own way deepens a parent's respect for their independence. Where there are mutual respect and shared values, parents and children can discuss many topics, such as family relationships, more intimately and honestly. The loosening of constraints allows parents and children to relax and have fun together. What could be more pleasant than a son or daughter inviting a parent for Shabbat dinner or out to lunch? Sandy says of her move back home, "We have an unusual and ideal relationship. We are more like roommates now than mother and daughter. We know our respective roles, but we have a friendship, and we live our own lives."

Taking the long view, remembering that young adulthood is a time of experiment, helps parents realize that their child's choices may be temporary. In Steve's words, "I look back now and see I wasn't mature enough to decide some things for myself. For instance, I understand why Shabbat dinner and Jewish holidays with the family were so important to my parents. Now that we don't see each other as much, I appreciate those opportunities for family closeness."

"What we must learn is how to let our children go while helping them at a later date to come back," say Strassfeld and Green in *The Jewish Family Book*. "We also want to have the courage and flexibility to go to our children," they continue, as the elderly Jacob undertook the arduous journey to Egypt to be reunited with his son Joseph more than two decades after they were separated.

"The only two lasting bequests we can give to our children," said an unknown writer, are "roots and wings." Parents can teach and model good values and judgment *and* trust their children.

Advice from Adult Children to Parents

1. Communicate. Discuss your expectations and plan ahead when an adult child comes home. Consult him about his own plans.

2. Respect each other's privacy. Knock on closed doors, call ahead instead of dropping in, avoid telephoning at inopportune times such as during work hours.

Advice from Parents to Adult Children

1. Avoid taking advantage of each other. Accept adult responsibilities like doing your own laundry and helping with the cooking when you come home. Let parents know when to expect you, and call if you'll be late.

2. Maintain contact. Share happy times as well as sad ones. Keep family members up-to-date so they can share and support.

Advice from Parents to Parents

1. See how your children handle independence *before* leaving home by curtailing control and instruction-giving by the time they are seniors in high school.

2. Putting children in charge of many decisions in their lives may prevent them from breaking loose and abusing freedom when they are on their own.

3. Remember yourself at that age. Develop reasonable expectations for your adult children in the context of their generation in today's world.

L'Dor Va-Dor: From Generation to Generation

What's the status symbol for the older generation these days? It's a child safety seat in your car. With this sign of active involvement, you don't even need that bumper sticker declaring: "If I had known grandchildren were so much fun, I would have had them first!"

"Simply becoming grandparents can open creative floodgates for elders to use the gift of time, health, and vitality, and to gain love and respect," says Arthur Kornhaber, M.D., a child psychiatrist and family therapist who has written about grandparents and their families in *Grandparents/Grandchildren—The Vital Connection, Between Parents and Grandparents,* and other works. Furthermore, Kornhaber asserts, "a healthy and loving bond between grandparents and grandchildren is necessary for the emotional health and happiness of all *three* generations."[1]

In advanced countries of the world today, more than 70% of people over age 65 are grandparents. Nearly half of these grandparents will live to become great-grandparents. Many older people today are still in the work force, and more enjoy greater financial security than their own struggling immigrant parents had. Other social changes affecting grandparents include expanded gender roles and greater mobility, resulting in the geographical dispersion of family members.

[1]Reprinted by permission of Transaction Publishers. *Grandparents, Grandchildren: The Vital Connection* by Arthur Kornhaber, M.D. Copyright 1991 by Transaction, New Brunswick, N.J.; all rights reserved.

Of those grandparents who live in the same community as their grandchildren, more are involved in the daily care and raising of grandchildren today than in the past. Cutting across all economic strata, this change is the result of several phenomena, including financial strains that have necessitated two parents' working, an increase in single-parent homes because of divorce, and the need for support to some parents with emotional problems.

"I knew only one of my four grandparents," muses one grandmother wistfully; "this created a void in my life." Today, thanks to greater longevity and sometimes economic necessity, the three generations have opportunities for relationships that were not so available in the past. At the same time, these changes present challenges for all involved.

The grandparent-grandchild relationship holds incredible richness. For the grandparent, it means continuity. Think of the moving scene in the last portion of Genesis (chapter 48) when Jacob summons all his sons to his deathbed to give them his final blessings. Jacob is overjoyed when Joseph arrives with his sons, Manasseh and Ephraim. He tells Joseph, "I had not thought to see your face; and lo, God has let me see your seed also." Using his God-given name, Israel, he adopts his grandsons, Ephraim and Manasseh, on the spot, thereby elevating them to a status equal to all his sons, and he blesses them even before their father Joseph, or any of his other offspring.

The beautiful blessing Israel gives his grandsons concludes: "and let my name be named in them, and the name of my fathers Abraham and Isaac, and let them grow into a multitude in the midst of the earth." Subsequent generations have linked themselves with Jacob's desire for continuity; to this day, parents bless their sons on Shabbat evening with the words, "God make you as Ephraim and as Manasseh."

Of course, continuity goes beyond genetic heritage. As one grandfather put it, "We like to see the chain of family traditions carried on." Grandparents transmit values from the past in many ways, such as language, family rituals, and even tools, recipes, and utensils. What more potent symbols of this continuity are there than Bubbie lighting Shabbos candles, Zayde leading the Passover Seder, or the Bar Mitzvah boy wearing his grandfather's *tallit?* For the child, a grandparent is a living historian, a valuable source of information about how things used to be, a window expanding his vision into other ways of thinking.

Grandparents are role models and teachers of ethics, morals, religion, and culture. This vital influence is captured beautifully in a children's book by Phyllis Rose Eisenberg, *A Mitzvah Is Something Special,* where a grandmother teaches her granddaughter, Lisa, about *mitzvot.*

Dr. Kornhaber portrays grandparents as nurturers, offering children unconditional love and acceptance in an unpressured atmosphere, benevolent authority, and a sanctuary when their parents falter. Other special roles they play, he says, are hero, wizard ("the boss's boss," as one child expressed it), and crony. Indeed, one of the biggest treats to a child is sleeping over at Grandma and Grandpa's house, with all the little traditions, privileges, and bending of the usual rules that this entails.

Finally, grandparents significantly influence a child's attitudes about older people, their own aging process and that of their parents, their future behavior as grandparents, and ultimately even about death. Dr. Kornhaber found that children who benefit from close relationships with their grandparents appreciate old people, view caring for family members as natural, and feel emotionally secure as individuals and as members of their family and community.

Grandparents are important to children in different ways as needed at different times in their lives. Children also realize that each grandparent plays certain roles better than others. In *A Mitzvah Is Something Special,* Lisa recognizes that while her two grandmothers are very different, they both love her.

Grandma Esther calls Lisa "Bubelah," which means "little grandmother." Bubbie, Nana, Grandma, Savta, Zayde, Pop-Pop—the individuality of each is reflected in the names *they* choose to be called, names which often carry warm memories and associations that are transmitted through the generations.

It is sad and ironic, however, that, although grandparents are living longer, many families are not enjoying the benefits of the inter-generational relationship. Dr. Kornhaber attributes this change to a lack of awareness of the importance of these bonds, the fact that people are choosing to spend more time with their peers, and a hectic pace impeding the formation of close attachments. He also sees a "new social contract, that grandparents and parents will have complete independence, . . . an unstated agreement which assures emotional isolation from each other."

How has this alienation of some adults from their parents come about? Some grandparents deliberately keep their distance, showing little interest in their grandchildren and not offering help. "We've fulfilled our duties as parents," say Sarah and Jerry; "now we want to enjoy life and freedom in our retirement years." Another reason some older people remain uninvolved is that they fear being exploited by their adult children for babysitting and other forms of care. Others feel insecure about assuming responsibility for young children. And some simply assume their involvement isn't welcome.

Such withdrawal by grandparents may hurt their children's and grandchildren's feelings and create resentment, say Lissy Jarvik, M.D. and Gary Small, M.D., authors of *Parentcare: A Commonsense Guide for Adult Children*. On the other hand, adult children sometimes discourage their parents' involvement because of changes in child-rearing practices and values. They worry, for example, about different methods of discipline, or about grandparents "spoiling" the children. Many adult children perceive their parents—even with the best of intentions—as criticizing their parenting, interfering, or undermining their authority. Thus, they may push away their older parents, giving them the message that they are not needed.

These frictions, say Drs. Jarvik and Small, can have serious repercussions for all the generations. Often at the heart of these struggles lie unresolved parent-child issues that predate the grandchildren. Adult children may vow to parent differently, only to find themselves repeating some of their parents' behavior.

An important key to resolving these conflicts is the awareness that parents are "the linchpin of the connection between grandparents and grandchildren," according to Dr. Kornhaber, whose study showed that "parents benefit when a close emotional attachment exists between their parents and their children." Arriving at this awareness requires communication. Adult children and their parents need to speak to each other, to make known their needs, feelings, and reasons for acting as they do. It is best not to use children to criticize or communicate indirectly with grandparents or parents.

Direct dialogue among adults in the family can lead to better understanding and acceptance of each other. Consulting a professional counselor or a rabbi can be helpful. Each party may have to bend a little. For example, parents can try to find specific ways in which grandparents can contribute and feel needed and appreciated. Ultimately, however, decisions affecting the children rest with the parents.

In long-distance relationships, this communication takes some special efforts. Irving and Doris, who live on the opposite coast from their grandchildren, write letters directly to them and call regularly. They stress the important role the middle generation plays in building the relationship by making sure the children respond to their grandparents' mail. Says their 7-year-old grandson, "I wish they could come to my class on Grandparents' Day. It's very special for me to see them because it's only a couple of times a year. I feel good when I get to talk to my grandparents on the phone, or get a letter, or best of all, see them in person."

Relationships are dynamic, and we need to keep ourselves open to the changes. Dealing with the challenges of inter-generational relationships can also be a path to discovering their possibilities and benefits. A grandmother at her grandson's Bar Mitzvah summed up the joys of grandparenting when she quoted a teaching from the Talmud: "*To hear your child's child reading Torah is like hearing the words from Sinai itself.*"[1]

Putting the *Grand* Back in Grandparenting

For grandchildren:

Get to know your grandparents while you have them. They are a living connection with the past.

---

[1]Cited in Rabbi Jeffrey K. Salkin, *Putting God on the Guest List: How to Reclaim the Spiritual Meaning of Your Child's Bar or Bat Mitzvah.* Woodstock, VT: Jewish Lights Publishing, 1992.

For parents:

Give your parents and your children time to themselves to foster the development of a unique relationship.

For grandparents:

Take advantage of opportunities to share experiences with your grandchildren such as outings to museums and concerts, volunteer *tzedakah* work, synagogue attendance, school activities, and inter-generational learning programs.

The Book Is Never Closed: Grandparents Dealing with the Repercussions of Divorce and Intermarriage

Diane has just told her parents, Stella and Jack, that her divorce has been finalized. Twelve years of marriage and a painful struggle over child custody have ended. Like Diane, Stella and Jack have many emotions during this passage in her life. They are particularly concerned about the impact of the divorce on their grandchildren.

Lainie and Arthur's son Stuart married Lynn, who is Catholic, five years ago. Religious observance has not been part of the young couple's home life, except that they do celebrate both Chanukah and Christmas. Now Stuart and Lynn's first child has been born. Lainie and Arthur wonder what their role will be in their grandson's life.

Divorce and intermarriage: each presents families with a unique set of challenges and issues. Yet there are some common threads connecting these two situations. For one, parents of an adult child who intermarries, like parents of an adult child who divorces, often perceive their child's choice as precipitating a crisis in the family. Indeed, divorce and intermarriage affect all three generations. There are repercussions for the relationships between parents and their adult children, as well as for those children's spouses and *their* fami-

188

lies. Also affected are the relationships between grandparents and grandchildren.

Intermarriage and divorce affect more Jewish families today than ever before. 52% of all Jews marrying today are intermarrying, according to the 1990 National Jewish Population Survey of the Council of Jewish Federations. About 37% of Jewish marriages today end in divorce. About half of all intermarriages end in divorce. Many re-marriages after divorce are also intermarriages. This is not the world in which today's grandparents grew up, and most are not prepared to deal with these kinds of changes in families, nor with the flood of complex feelings that they unleash.

When Diane first told her parents that she and her husband were separating, Stella and Jack were shocked. "What happened?" they asked. "We thought you two were so happy." Like many adult children, Diane had not shared her marital problems with her parents, so the announcement of the separation left them feeling bewildered and, in some way, guilty. "Could we have done something more to support our daughter and son-in-law's marriage?" they wondered.

As the finality sank in, Stella and Jack felt a deep sense of loss—of their expectations and dreams for their daughter's marriage and future. They also felt the loss of their warm relationship with Diane's husband as well as a sense of hurt and betrayal. Was he not the person they had thought? Their cordial relationship with the in-laws became strained. Even more painful was losing their free access to their grandchildren, for now they would all be forced to adhere to an arbitrary schedule set by a judge.

Loss, guilt, confusion, powerlessness—grandparents, parents, *and* children experience these feelings when divorce occurs. Families affected by intermarriage go through similar reactions and feelings. For example, parents whose children intermarry often feel that they somehow failed to give their children a solid enough Jewish identity.

What particularly concerns grandparents in both situations is that they may lose the opportunity to hand down the values they cherish. Grandchildren are their bridge to the future, but many grandparents feel that their adult children's choices have set up roadblocks, depriving them of the opportunity to pass on important traditions and beliefs.

People whose child intermarries also have a unique concern. For Lainie and Arthur, this was already on their minds from the moment Stuart got engaged (in fact, it went back to the time when he began dating). It's a fear that their grandchildren will be significantly different, and that the gap between them will be too wide to bridge. The dilemma for these grandparents is how to transmit their heritage to their interfaith grandchildren without alienating their own adult child and the non-Jewish spouse.

To help grandparents like Lainie and Arthur, Sunie Levin, an educator who is herself a grandparent, has written *Mingled Roots: A Guide for Jewish Grandparents of Interfaith Children.* Commissioned by B'nai B'rith Women, the book posits that grandparents are "the nurturers of religious faith and values; as such, they have a special opportunity to build relationships that will help strengthen the Jewish heritage of their grandchildren."

Because of the potential for conflict and a fear of alienation, however, religious faith often becomes a taboo subject between parents and their adult children who intermarry. Levin counsels parents to open communication about religion, approaching it with diplomacy. Parents may disagree with their adult child's choices about his own religious identity and that of the grandchildren. But they will have a better relationship with their children and grandchildren if they accept and *respect* these choices and are sensitive to their feelings.

It is also important that grandparents consult with the parents to define guidelines about what ways of sharing their heritage with the grandchildren are acceptable. "Your entire purpose is to give the child a better sense of who he is, where he comes from, what his roots are," says Levin.

Yours is not the only heritage being passed down to your grandchildren, Levin points out. Let them know you recognize that all of their relatives are part of their lives, and that different beliefs must be respected. However, you should be clear and honest about what you believe. What you do is as important as what you say. Children can learn about positive commitment to Judaism by seeing their grandparents practice these values in everyday life. The main role of grandparents is "to provide, through settings such as Jewish holiday celebrations in the home, opportunities for displaying the richness of the Jewish heritage in the context of warm family ties," says David G. Sacks, president of the Jewish Outreach Institute, in "Welcoming the Intermarried into Your Jewish Family." Grandparents also serve as connections to Jewish institutions and resources.

An adult child's choice to intermarry sometimes prompts self-exploration in the parents, who may look at their own identity and discover that Judaism means more to them than they had realized. Identity is an evolving process. All three generations are travellers on this journey, and life cycle changes such as beginning college, marriage, the birth of a child, or the death of a loved one can stimulate self-discovery and growth. As one rabbi put it, "the book is never closed."

The non-Jewish fiancé or spouse, who will or has become your son- or daughter-in-law, has embarked on a journey, too—a journey which potentially could lead to conversion. "But because Judaism is not currently an active proselytizing religion, it remains up to the family to be the initial catalyst in stimulating thinking, discussion, and initiative regarding conversion," says David Sacks. He recommends taking a welcoming and informative approach governed by "warmth, respect, and sensitivity."

Catherine Hall Myrowitz, author of *Finding a Home for the Soul: Interviews with Converts to Judaism,* says that the response of the family is a significant factor, though not the *only* one, in a person's desire to convert. Through her own experience and those of other Jews-by-Choice who tell their stories in the book, she concluded that "the best way to make being a Jew attractive to someone else is to be the best Jew you can, living a vibrant Jewish life, and to be warm and embracing to others." For example, suggests Myrowitz, if you are making gefilte fish or challah, invite your daughter-in-law to come over and participate, or ask if she'd like to attend a meeting of your Jewish book group or a Hadassah program.

If your adult child's fiancé or spouse has converted, or is in the process of conversion, look carefully at your attitudes. Many Jews do not realize, or find it difficult to accept, the fact that converts are "genuine, legitimate Jews," many of whom have learned more about Judaism than some people born to the religion, says Lawrence J. Epstein in *Conversion to Judaism: A Guidebook.* Dr. Epstein describes the most fortunate convert as "one who can use an in-law as a role model, asking questions, and receiving support and help."

"A person who converts to Judaism does not thereby instantly acquire the kind of Jewish ethnicity that belongs to most of us—religious or not—who are Jews at birth," says David Sacks of The Jewish Outreach Institute. "Becoming Jewish is a process that Jewish families can and ought to nurture," Sacks continues. "Therefore, Jewish family members must play a supportive role so as to ease the socialization and acculturation of a newly Jewish family member into the ways of the Jewish community."

When adult children have chosen to follow either no religious tradition, or one other than Judaism, respecting each others' decisions and feelings may demand much effort. It is important to acknowledge one's feelings of loss, and to talk to a friend, spouse, rabbi, or counselor. Joining a support group with others who have similar experiences is also helpful. Often spouses do not react in the same ways to their children's choices; a support group can help them strengthen their own bond.

Paying attention to feelings and seeking support are also important for parents whose children have divorced. Blaming your adult child will cause pain and is unproductive. Offer your support by listening, giving advice only when asked, and helping out when you can. If you extend financial help, make the terms clear, and avoid attaching strings or expectations.

Grandparents can be a vital source of support to grandchildren experiencing the emotional turmoil of their parents' divorce. Through unconditional warmth and love, grandparents can provide a sense of security. Take your cues from the child about how much he or she wants to discuss the family situation.

At the heart of the reactions to the changes brought by divorce and intermarriage is the relationship between parents and their adult children. Divorce and intermarriage magnify the existing parent-child relationship. If it was already strained, it is likely to become more tense. If it was good, it has the potential to become stronger.

Intermarriage and divorce can exacerbate tensions in families or create new ones. These changes force family members to re-examine relationships they may have taken for granted. Like every individual, every relationship carries within it the potential for growth. The key is to focus on what you *can* do, and to seek common ground. Changes can be opportunities for parents and their adult children to clarify what is really important to them, and for all three generations to build the most fulfilling relationships they can with each other.

Bridging the Gaps Between Generations

1. If divorce or intermarriage occur in your family, acknowledge your own feelings of loss, and seek support to help you deal with them.

2. Try to keep an open mind and open lines of communication with your children and grandchildren.

3. Remember that you can still play a positive role in the lives of your children and grandchildren. In the case of intermarriage, if adult children have decided to raise the grandchildren as Jews, grandparents can be active participants in shaping the grandchildren's Jewish identity, especially if they live nearby. This role is harder to perform when the children live at a distance, but grandparents can communicate by phone calls and visits, and by sending letters, tapes, books, and gifts.

4. Avoid disparaging another faith or comparing Jewish, non-Jewish, and interfaith members of the family.

5. When your adult child has divorced, avoid speaking negatively or asking your grandchild for information about the other parent, and don't take sides. Respect the bond that still exists between that parent and your grandchild.

Parenting Our Parents

The Yom Kippur liturgy contains a powerful appeal to God: "Do not cast us off in our old age, nor forsake us when our strength fails." "Every year," says Ben, "when we get to that place in the service, my mother nudges me with her elbow, reminding me—with a smile only half in jest—of my filial duty."

Volumes have been written on the fifth commandment, "Honor thy father and thy mother." The rabbis equated observance of this *mitzvah* with the fear of God, and promised rewards both in this world and the world to come. But Rabbi Simeon bar Yochai (Tanhuma, Ekev 2) and other sages also recognized it as one of the most difficult of God's commandments because of the awesome responsibility of the task—particularly as parents age.

There is an old saying that one mother can take care of ten children, but ten children cannot take care of one mother. Nothing could be farther from the truth. In fact, most "elder care" today is provided by family members. The majority of these are daughters and daughters-in-law, who assume responsibilities ranging from the simplest of tasks to complex personal care. They have become the primary caregivers of the elderly.

Caregivers fill a wide variety of roles. They include the daughter who stops by her parents' home after work each evening to help them get ready for bed, the out-of-town children who alternate visiting parents on weekends to help arrange and manage care for them, and the son who now writes checks and handles other financial matters for his mildly confused father.

But caregiving is not without considerable problems. Past generations and biology established the pattern that parents take care of children, not the reverse. It is only in very recent times that medical science has increased life expectancy so that people over age 65 are the fastest growing segment of our population. However, along with the blessing of added years has come an increase in chronic illnesses with their often dreaded companion: dependency.

Caring for an elderly parent may feel unnatural to both the adult child and the elderly parent, who cherishes independence. Society has defined the parent's role as provider of food, clothing, and protection. Now the one who has made the world safe for us in the past, in turn, needs to be cared for. This apparent role reversal challenges our sense of filial maturity since we worked so hard at growing up and developing a relationship to our parents as adult to adult.

Many grown children are singularly unprepared when a mother's or father's needs demand this new parenting cycle. We tend to take our parents' presence and functioning for granted until they become ill. Because we are usually middle-aged when this occurs, we are abruptly reminded of our own mortality. At the same time we often have feelings ranging from anger at this added burden, to guilt for daring to harbor such "alien" thoughts. Revealing their understanding of human nature, the rabbis specified that aid to a needy parent must be given with a generous spirit, not grudgingly. Abimi the son of Rabbi Abahu taught: "A man may feed his father pheasant, and [yet] be driven from the world [to come] . . ." The great medieval commentator Rashi interprets being "driven from the world" as "he is punished . . . for he displays a mean spirit as he feeds him [his father]."

Lissy Jarvik, M.D. and Gary Small, M.D., geropsychiatrists and authors of *Parentcare: A Commonsense Guide for Adult Children,* have written: "The extraordinary stress of caring for children and parents—simultaneously or sequentially—is a phenomenon of our times." "Women in the middle" and "the sandwich generation" are phrases which have entered our vocabulary to describe this increasingly common life cycle event. Adding to the crunch are the growing number of children who live at great geographic distances from parents and the escalation of the number of women in the work force.

Being wedged between the needs of children and those of parents can cause considerable stress.

Sharon, a widow with a teenage daughter, moved back to her home town to be closer to her mother who had become physically frail and sometimes forgetful. At first she gave willingly of her time and energy—helping her mother with shopping, meal preparation, and transportation. Soon Sharon's full-time job and the demands of raising her own daughter took their toll. Physically and emotionally exhausted, she began to resent having to provide support and sustenance to her mother. Without really understanding why, she kept recalling instances during her childhood when she felt her mother was not providing the nurturing she desired. Sharon's feeling of being overburdened was increased by the fact that her only sister lived out-of-state and offered no help.

Sharon sought relief by turning to her Jewish Family Service agency. Counseling helped her cope with her feelings of worry, resentment, and guilt. Sharon came to see that her mother had done the best job of nurturing that she could. She learned the importance of treating our parents as adults, of accepting them as human beings who happen to be our parents.

Unlike child care, which involves making a temporary arrangement leading to the greater independence of the child, parent care is a much more complex process occurring over a long time, with the outcome being greater dependence of the parent on the child. A family member caring for an elderly parent may need help in understanding the changes that aging brings, the complex problems and the multiple services necessary to deal with them, as well as assistance with gaining access to those services.

For example, in addition to counseling, Sharon was able to utilize affordable agency services, including a geriatric evaluation of her mother and consultation to explore options for her care. Homemaker services, escorts for shopping and medical appointments, and friendly visitors were also provided.

Counseling helped Sharon outline a strategy to include her sister in planning, along with her mother, with the goal of enabling their mother to maintain the greatest possible degree of independence and involvement in decisions affecting her life. As a result of this help, Sharon's feelings of being overwhelmed were alleviated and her commitments to her mother, her child, and her job became more manageable.

Many older parents never need extensive, long-term help from their children. However, some do need ongoing care. We can no sooner desert our parents in their old age than they could abandon us when we were children. Reciprocally satisfactory solutions are needed.

The rabbis of the Talmud teach: "What is the reverence and honor [due to parents]? Reverence means that a child must not stand or sit in his parent's place, nor contradict his words, nor tip the scale against him. Honor means that the child must provide the parent with food and drink, clothe and cover him, and lead him in and out" [in old age and infirmity]. (Talmud Kiddushin 31b) Throughout the tradition, Judaism emphasizes the requirement to provide direct acts of service to parents as an expression of love and devotion, while at the same time remaining sensitive to their dignity as parents. As much as elderly parents may become like children to their children, Judaism reminds us that our parents are always our parents, and we must be ever cognizant of the special respect they deserve.

Another old adage says: You can't be human alone. Caregiving can be a shared task which draws from the resources of family and community and which strengthens our bonds with both.

Suggestions on Caring for Elderly Parents

1. Whenever possible, consult your older parent about, and consider, his or her wishes, needs, and capabilities.

2. Advance planning can avert crises and confusion. Gather information about resources and options in the community with the help of agencies such as Jewish Family Services.

3. Involve as many members of the family as possible in discussions and decision-making.

4. Build in respite from your caregiving responsibilities through support groups, help from others, and time for yourself.

Collaborators:
Jewish Family Services
of Central Maryland

Eve Berkow, RNCS-P, LCSW-C, is a psychiatric clinical nurse specialist and a social worker at Jewish Family Services.

Talking with Your Child About Sexuality

Nancy Silver Britcher, LCSW-C, was on the staff of JFS Older Adult Services from 1992–1994.

The Power of Laughter

Harry Citron, LCSW-C, is director of Older Adult Services at JFS.

Parenting Our Parents

L'Dor Va-Dor: From Generation to Generation

Joan Grayson Cohen, Esq., LCSW-C, is director of the JFS Child Abuse and Neglect Prevention Program.

The Art of Positive Discipline

The Nuts and Bolts of Positive Discipline

Shana Goldfinger, LCSW-C, is on the staff of Older Adult Services of JFS.

Making the High Holidays Meaningful for Children

Passover: Opening the Door to Children's Questions

Susan Goldstein, LCSW-C, is director of Child, Adolescent, and Adult Services at JFS.

Fears about School

When Parenting Feels Like an Overwhelming Job

Beth Land Hecht, LCSW-C, is on the staff of Child, Adolescent, and Adult Services of JFS and directs the Jewish Outreach Network: Programs for Jews By Choice and Those Affected by Intermarriage, a joint project of JFS and the Baltimore Board of Rabbis.

The Family with a Difference: Children with Disabilities

The Book Is Never Closed: Grandparents Dealing with the Repercussions of Divorce and Intermarriage

So Many Hamans . . . Helping Young Children Respond to Anti-Semitism

Myra L. Hettleman, LCSW-C, is associate director of JFS Children's Services and director of Adoption Alliances of JFS.

Surviving Summer Camp

Joseph M. Honsberger, LCSW-C, is a social worker and clinical supervisor at the JFS district office in Owings Mills, Maryland.

To Tell or Not to Tell?

Rachel Howard, LCSW, is director of Residential and Support Services of JFS.

Teaching Children to Appreciate Differences

Irene Jordan, LCSW-C, was on the staff of Children's Services of JFS from 1980 to 1994. From 1988 to 1994 she was an adoption specialist and then associate director of JFS' Adoption Alliances.

Adoption: Another Way to Grow a Family

Alice Kolman, MSW, is director of Jewish Family Life Programs of JFS.

Escaping from the Body Trap

Mimi B. Kraus, LCSW-C, is assistant director of JFS Child, Adolescent and Adult Services and site manager at the JFS district office in Owings Mills, Maryland.

Gifts of Love

Joan Kristall, LCSW-C, is on the staff of Child, Adolescent, and Adult Services of JFS, and directs the agency's Programs for Families of Separation, Divorce and Remarriage.

The Book is Never Closed: Grandparents Dealing with the Repercussions of Divorce and Intermarriage

Are we Overprogramming Our Children?

Pulling Together after Coming Apart: Life Cycle Events forFamilies of Divorce

The "X" Factor: How Parents' New Relationships after Divorce Affect the Children

Janet Kurland, LCSW-C, is associate director of Older Adult Services at JFS.

Parenting Our Parents

L'Dor Va-Dor: From Generation to Generation

Helen Landry, LCSW, was on the staff of Child, Adolescent, and Adult Services of JFS from 1989 to 1993.

Of Turkey and Tension

Ben Levey, LCSW-C, is on the staff of Children's Services and directs the Miriam Project for child foster care of JFS.

Focus on Fatherhood

Beverly C. Nackman, LCSW-C, was associate director of Adolescent and Adult Services at JFS, where she worked from 1971–1996.

Holding On and Letting Go: How to Build a Healthy Relationship with Your Adult Child

Ellen Schwartz Patterson, LCSW-C, was a social worker at the JFS district office in Owings Mills, Maryland, from 1989–1995.

Even "Normal" Families Need Help Now and Then

Barbara Perry, LCSW, worked in Children's Services at JFS from 1991–1993.

When Your Child Doesn't Fit In

Rhoda K. Posner, LCSW-C, was district director and then assistant director for special programs in JFS Child, Adolescent, and Adult Services from 1991–1997.

Money Matters

Barbara S. Ringel, LCSW-C, is a social worker and clinical supervisor with Children's Services of JFS.

Sibling Struggles

Falling Stars and Earthly Models

Is It Love or Is It Spoiling?

Mary Sachs, RNC, is the community health nurse at JFS, with a specialty in psychiatry.

Escaping from the Body Trap

Merle D. Sachs, LCSW-C, is a clinical supervisor in Child, Adolescent, and Adult Services and coordinates the School Consultation Program of JFS.

Fears About School

Lucy Y. Steinitz, Ph.D., was Executive Director of Jewish Family Services of Central Maryland from 1983–1996, and director of Client Services at JFS from 1981–1983.

The One and Only

Myra Strassler, LCSW-C, is on the staff of the Child, Adolescent, and Adult Services department of JFS.

Making the High Holidays Meaningful for Children

Debra K. Waranch, LCSW-C, is a social worker and clinical supervisor with Child, Adolescent, and Adult Services of JFS.

The December Dilemma

Making the Most of Summer

Dealing with Rejection

Marci B. Dickman, Executive Director of Baltimore's Council on Jewish Education Services, contributed to the chapter *Teaching Children to Appreciate Differences.*

Rena Rotenberg, MA, director of Early Childhood Education of the Council on Jewish Education Services, contributed to the chapter *Making the High Holidays Meaningful for Children.*

Resources

The One and Only

Abrams, Rabbi Judith Z. and Dr. Steven A. Abrams. *Jewish Parenting: Rabbinic Insights*. Northvale, N.J.: Jason Aronson, Inc., 1994.

Lamm, Maurice. *The Jewish Way in Love and Marriage*. Middle Village, New York: Jonathan David Publishers, Inc., 1980.

McGrath, Ellie. *My One and Only: The Special Experience of the Only Child*. New York: William Morrow and Company, Inc., 1989.

Newman, Susan. *Parenting an Only Child*. New York: Doubleday and Company, Inc., 1990.

Peck, Ellen. *The Joy of the Only Child*. New York: Delacorte Press, 1977.

Simons, Harriet Fishman. *Wanting Another Child: Coping with Secondary Infertility*. New York: Lexington Books, 1995.

Sibling Struggles

Faber, Adele and Elaine Mazlish. *Siblings Without Rivalry*. New York: Norton, 1987.

Klagsbrun, Francine. *Mixed Feelings: Love, Hate, Rivalry and Reconciliation Among Brothers and Sisters*. New York: Bantam Books, 1993.

McDermott, John, M.D. *The Complete Book on Sibling Rivalry.* New York, N.Y.: Wideview Books (Division of Putnam), 1980.

Salk, Lee. *What Every Child Would Like His Parents to Know.* New York: David McKay and Co., 1972.

Strassfeld, Sharon and Kathy Green. *The Jewish Family Book.* New York: Bantam Books, 1981. "Sibling Rivalry," pp. 225–232.

Adoption: Another Way to Grow a Family

Adoptive Families of America, 3333 Highway 100 N., Minneapolis, MN 55422.

Brodzinsky, David M. et al. *Being Adopted: The Lifelong Search for Self.* New York: Anchor Books, Doubleday, 1993.

Gold, Rabbi Michael. *And Hannah Wept: Infertility, Adoption and the Jewish Couple.* Dunmore, PA: Jewish Publication Society, 1988.

McPherson, Carolyn Flanders and Hillel Rosenfeld. "Let's Celebrate Adoption: A Guide for the Jewish Community." The Center Source, Spaulding for Children, 16250 Northland Dr., Suite 120, Southfield, MI 48075.

Melina, Lois Ruskai. *Making Sense of Adoption: A Parent's Guide.* New York: Harper & Row Publishers, 1989.

Melina, Lois Ruskai. *Raising Adopted Children: A Manual for Adoptive Parents.* New York: Harper and Row, Publishers, 1986.

Stars of David International, Inc., information and support network for Jewish and partly Jewish adoptive families, 3175 Commercial Ave., Suite 100, Northbrook, IL 60062-1915.

Stein, Sara Bonnett. *The Adopted One: An Open Family Book for Parents and Children Together.* New York: Walker and Company, 1979.

Children's Literature

Brodzinsky, Anne Braff. *The Mulberry Bird: Story of an Adoption.* Indianapolis, Indiana: Perspectives Press, 1986.

Freudberg, Judy and Tony Geiss. *Susan and Gordon Adopt a Baby.* New York: Random House, Inc., Children's Television Workshop, 1986.

Koch, Janice. *Our Baby: A Birth and Adoption Story.* Indianapolis, Indiana: Perspectives Press, 1985.

Krementz, Jill. *How It Feels to Be Adopted.* New York: Alfred A. Knopf, 1982.

Pellegrini, Nina. *Families Are Different.* New York: Holiday House, 1991.

Roseman, Kenneth. *All in My Jewish Family.* New York: Union of American Hebrew Congregations, 1984.

Rosenberg, Maxine B. *Being Adopted.* New York: Lothrop, Lee and Shepard Books, 1984.

Schaeffer, Patricia. *Chag Sameach! A Jewish Holiday Book for Children.* Berkeley, CA: Tabor Sarah Books.

Simon, Norma. *All Kinds of Families.* Morton Grove, Illinois: Albert Whitman and Company, 1976.

———. *Why Am I Different?* Morton Grove, Illinois: Albert Whitman and Company, 1976.

The Family with a Difference: Children with Disabilities

Child and Family Support Program, Kennedy Krieger Institute, 2911 E. Biddle Street, Baltimore, MD 21213, (410) 550-9700.

Department of Special Education, Council on Jewish Education Services, 5800 Park Heights Avenue, Baltimore, MD 21215, (410) 578-6946.

Exceptional Parent Magazine, P.O. Box 3000, Denville, NY 07834-9964.

Featherstone, Helen. *A Difference in the Family: Living with a Disabled Child.* New York: Basic Books, 1980.

Fingertips (a telephone guide to toll-free numbers of national organizations and agencies providing information for and about people with disabilities), Disability Resources, Inc., 4 Glatter Lane, Centereach, N.Y. 11720-1032.

Granger, Lori and Bill Granger. *The Magic Feather: The Truth About "Special Education."* New York: Dell Publishing, 1986.

The Jewish Braille Institute of America, 110 East 30 St., New York, NY 10016.

The Jewish Heritage for the Blind, 1655 E. 24 Street, Brooklyn, NY 11229.

Levine, Dr. Mel. *Keeping a Head in School: A Student's Book about Learning Abilities and Learning Disorders.* Cambridge, Massachusetts: Educators Publishing Service, 1990.

"Liheyot," Union of American Hebrew Congregations Education Department, 838 Fifth Avenue, New York, NY 10021 (produces a national newsletter for families of children with special needs, organizes sensitivity workshops, and develops curricula for synagogues).

Maryland Association for Jewish Parents of Children with Disabilities, Marjorie Shulbank, (410) 225-4269.

National Center for Learning Disabilities, Inc. 99 Park Avenue South, New York, N.Y. 10016 (212) 545-7510.

National Conference of Synagogue Youth, 333 7th Avenue, New York, NY 10001 (212) 563-4000. "Our Way"—for children who are deaf. "Yachad"—National Council for the Disabled.

Quinn, Patricia O., M.D., and Judith M. Stern, M.A. *Brakes: The Interactive Newsletter for Kids with ADD.* Magination Press, 9 Union Square West, New York, N.Y. 10003, (800) 825-3039.

——— and Judith M. Stern, M.A. *Putting on the Brakes: Young People's Guide to Understanding Attention Deficit Hyperactivity Disorder,* and *The "Putting on the Brakes" Activity Book for Young People with ADHD.* Brunner/Mazel, 19 Union Square West, New York, N.Y. 10003, (212) 924-3344.

Shuart, Adele Kronick. *Signs in Judaism: A Resource Book for the Jewish Deaf Community.* New York: Bloch Publishing, 1986.

Smith, Sally L. *Succeeding Against the Odds: Strategies and Insights from the Learning Disabled.* Los Angeles, CA: Jeremy P. Tarcher, Inc., 1991.

Strassfeld, Sharon and Kathy Green. *The Jewish Family Book.* New York: Bantam Books, 1981. "Educating the Special Child," pp. 188–201.

Teaching Children to Appreciate Differences

Astor, Carl. . . . *Who Makes People Different: Jewish Perspectives on the Disabled.* New York: United Synagogue of America Youth Activities, 155 Fifth Avenue, New York, NY 10010, 1985.

"Dignity and Disability: A Jewish Discovery Kit." Board of Jewish Education of Greater Washington, 11710 Hunters Lane, Rockville, MD 20852.

"Justice, Justice for All: Promoting Disability Awareness in the Jewish Community." Greater Los Angeles Bureau of Jewish Education, 6505 Wilshire Blvd., Suite 710, Los Angeles, CA 90048.

"Kids on the Block," an educational puppet company. 9385-C Gerwig Lane, Columbia, MD 21046. 1-800-368-KIDS.

Children's Literature

Brightman, Alan. *Like Me.* Boston: Little, Brown and Company, 1976.

Brown, Tricia. *Someone Special, Just Like You.* New York: Henry Holt and Company, 1984.

Cohen, Floreva G. *My Special Friend.* New York: Board of Jewish Education of Greater New York, 1986.

Cohen, Miriam. *See You Tomorrow, Charles.* New York: Dell Publishing, 1983.

Gellman, Ellie. *Jeremy's Dreidel.* Rockville, MD: Kar-Ben Copies, Inc., 1993.

Klein, Gerda. *The Blue Rose.* Westport, CT: Lawrence Hill and Company, 1974.

Krementz, Jill. *How It Feels to Live with a Physical Disability.* New York: Simon and Schuster, 1992.

Peterson, Jeanne Whitehouse. *I Have a Sister, My Sister is Deaf.* New York: Harper Collins Children's Books, 1984.

Quinsey, Mary Beth. *Why Does That Man Have Such a Big Nose?* Seattle, Washington: Parenting Press, Inc., 1986.

Westridge Young Writers Workshop. *Kids Explore the Gifts of Children with Special Needs.* Santa Fe, N.M.: John Muir Publications, 1994.

Pulling Together After Coming Apart: Life Cycle Events for Families of Divorce

Ahrons, Constance R. *The Good Divorce: Keeping Your Family Together When Your Marriage Comes Apart.* New York: Harper, Collins Publishers, 1994.

Grollman, Earl. *Talking about Divorce: A Dialogue Between Parent and Child.* Boston: Beacon Press, 1975.

Kalter, Neil. *Growing Up with Divorce.* New York: Fawcett Columbine (A Division of Ballantine Books, Inc.), 1991.

Lamm, Maurice. *The Jewish Way in Love and Marriage.* Middle Village, New York: Jonathan David Publishers, Inc., 1980.

Lansky, Vicki. *Divorce Book for Parents: Helping Your Children Cope with Divorce and Its Aftermath.* Canada: Penguin Books, 1989.

Children's Literature

Blume, Judy. *Are You There, God? It's Me, Margaret.* New York: Dell Publishing Company, Inc., 1991.

Gardner, Richard A. *Boys and Girls Book About Divorce.* New York: Bantam Books, 1971.

———. *Boys and Girls Book About One-Parent Families.* Cresskill, N.J.: Creative Therapeutics, 1983.

Mayle, Peter. *Why Are We Getting a Divorce?* New York: Crown Publishing Group, Harmony Books, 1988.

Pomerantz, Barbara. *Who Will Lead Kiddush?* New York: Union of American Hebrew Congregations, 1985.

The X Factor: How Parents' New Relationships after Divorce Affect the Children

Bienenfeld, Florence. *Helping Your Child Succeed After Divorce.* Alameda, CA: Hunter House, Inc., 1987.

Cherlin, Andrew, and Frank J. Furstenberg, Jr. *Divided Families: What Happens to Children When Families Part.* Harvard University Press, 1991.

Diament, Carol, ed. *Jewish Marital Status.* A Hadassah Study. Northvale, N.J.: Jason Aronson, Inc., 1989.

Grollman, Earl A. *Talking About Divorce: A Dialogue Between Parent and Child*. Boston: Beacon Press, 1975.

Jarratt, Claudia Jewett. *Helping Children Cope with Separation and Loss*. Boston, Massachusetts: The Harvard Common Press, 1994.

Trafford, A. *Crazy Time*. New York: Harper Collins Publishers, 1992.

Wallerstein, Judith S. and Sandra Blakeslee. *Second Chances*. Ticknor and Fields, 1990.

—— and Joan Berlin Kelly. *Surviving the Break-up: How Children and Parents Cope with Divorce*. New York: Basic Books, 1990.

Fears about School

Garber, Stephen W., Ph.D. et al. *Monsters Under the Bed and Other Childhood Fears*. New York: Villard Books, 1993.

Gasson, I. John, Ph.D. *Helping Your Child Succeed at School*. Los Angeles: Warwick Publishing, 1995.

Kellerman, Jonathan, Ph.D. *Helping the Fearful Child*. Chicago: Contemporary Books, 1981.

National Association of School Psychologists, Michael Martin and Cynthia Waltman-Greenwood, eds. *Solve Your Child's School-Related Problems*. New York: Harper Perennial, a division of Harper Collins Publishers, 1995.

Rich, Dorothy. *Mega Skills: How Families Can Help Children Succeed in School and Beyond*. National Education Association Edition. Boston: Houghton Mifflin Company, 1988.

Rosemond, John. *Ending the Homework Hassle*. Kansas City, Missouri: Andrews & McMeel, 1990.

Children's Literature

Ahlberg, Janet and Alan. *Starting School*. New York: Viking Kestral, 1988.

Berenstein, Stan and Jan. *The Berenstein Bears Go to School*. New York: Random House, Inc., 1978.

Cohen, Miriam. *Will I Have a Friend?* New York, NY: The Macmillan Company, 1967.

Howe, James. *When You Go to Kindergarten.* New York: Morrow Junior Books, 1994.

Rodgers, Elizabeth. *Ollie Goes to School.* New York: Scholastic, Inc., 1992.

Stein, Sara Bonnet. *A Child Goes to School: A Storybook for Parents and Children Together.* Garden City, N.Y.: A Dolphin Book, Doubleday and Company, Inc., 1978.

When Your Child Doesn't Fit In

Ames, Louise Bates, Frances L. Ilg, Carol Chase Haber, et al. Books on child development from Gesell Institute of Human Development. New York: Dell Publishing Company.

Greenspan, Stanley, M.D. and Nancy Thorndike Greenspan. *First Feelings.* New York: Viking Penguin, Inc., 1985.

Zimbardo, Philip G. and Shirley Rado. *A Parent's Guide to the Shy Child.* New York: McGraw Hill Book Company, 1981.

Are We Overprogramming Our Children?

Ames, Louise Bates and Carol Chase. *Don't Push Your Preschooler.* Gesell Institute of Human Development. New York: Dell Publishing Company.

Bettelheim, Bruno. *A Good Enough Parent.* New York: Vintage Books, A Division of Random House, 1987. Chapters 14–18 on the importance of play.

Elkind, Dr. David. *The Hurried Child: Growing Up Too Fast Too Soon.* Redding, Massachusetts: Addison Wesley Publishing Co., Inc., 1988.

———. *Miseducation: Preschoolers at Risk.* New York: Alfred A. Knopf, Inc., 1987.

Marzollo, Jean and Janice Lloyd. *Learning Through Play.* New York: Harper & Row, Publishers, 1972.

Winnicott, D. W. "Why Children Play" in *The Child, The Family, and the Outside World.* New York: Viking Penguin, Inc., 1964.

Dealing with Rejection

Birnbaum, Eli & Menachem Persoff. *The Israel Yeshiva Guide for Overseas Students*. Orthodox Union—NCSY Publications, 333 7th Avenue, New York, N.Y. 10001, (212) 613-8226.

Goldberg, Dr. Lee & Lana Goldberg. *The Jewish Student's Guide to American Colleges*. Shapolsky Publishers, 136 W. 22 St., New York, N.Y. 10011, 1989.

Hillel Guide to Jewish Life on Campus: A Directory of Resources for Jewish College Students. B'nai B'rith Hillel Foundations, 1640 Rhode Island Avenue, N.W., Washington, DC 20036, (202) 857-6606, (202) 857-6597.

The Insider's Guide to Colleges, ed. *Yale Daily News*. New York: St. Martin's Press, published annually.

The Israel Experience—The 1996 Complete Guide, American Zionist Youth Foundation, 110 E. 59th Street, NY, NY 10022, 1-800-27-ISRAEL, (212) 339-6916, West Coast Office (213) 655-6804. For high school, college, and summer experiences.

Peterson's Guide to Four-Year Colleges. Princeton, N.J.: Peterson's, published annually.

Dr. Seuss. *Oh, The Places You'll Go!* New York: Random House, Inc., 1990.

Spencer, Janet & Sandra Maleson. *The Complete Guide to College Visits*. Secaucus, N.J.: Citadel Press Books, 1993.

Strassfeld, Sharon and Kathy Green. *The Jewish Family Book*. New York: Bantam Books, 1981. "After High School," "Jewish Life on Campus," pp. 354–364.

When Parenting Feels Like an Overwhelming Job

Child Abuse and Neglect Prevention Project. Jewish Family Services of Central Maryland. 5750 Park Heights Avenue, Baltimore, MD 21215. Joan G. Cohen, Esq., LCSW, Coordinator, (410) 466-9200.

"Child Abuse and Neglect: A Responsibility of the Jewish Community." Ohel Children's Home and Family Services, 4510 16th Avenue, Brooklyn, N.Y. 11204, (718) 851-6300.

Cohen, Joan Grayson. *Feeling Good, Being Safe: A Primer for the Pre-school Age Child*. Baltimore, MD: Jewish Family Services of Central Maryland, Inc., 1995.

————. *Playing It Safe With Your Child: Eli and Ellie Learn About Safety*. Baltimore, MD: Jewish Family Services of Central Maryland, Inc., 1994.

Faber, Adele and Mazlish, Elaine. *How to Talk So Kids Will Listen and Listen So Kids Will Talk*. New York: Avon Books, 1980.

Ginott, Dr. Haim G. *Between Parent and Child*. New York, N.Y.: The Macmillan Company, 1965.

Parents Anonymous, Inc. National office: 675 West Foothill Blvd., Suite 220, Claremont, CA 91711, (909) 621-6184 (has over 30 state offices).

"Plain Talk About Handling Stress" and "Plain Talk About The Art of Relaxation." National Institute of Mental Health, Division of Communications and Education, Plain Talk Series, Ruth Kay, Editor. U.S. Department of Health and Human Services, Alcohol, Drug Abuse, and Mental Health Administration, 5600 Fishers Lane, Rockville, MD 20857.

Siegler, Ava L., Ph.D. *What Should I Tell the Kids? A Parent's Guide to Real Problems in the Real World*. New York: NAL-Dutton, 1994.

The Art of Positive Discipline / The Nuts and Bolts of Positive Discipline

Abrams, Rabbi Judith Z. and Dr. Steven A. Abrams. *Jewish Parenting: Rabbinic Insights*. Northvale, N.J.: Jason Aronson, Inc., 1994.

Bettelheim, Dr. Bruno. *A Good Enough Parent*. N.Y.: Vintage Books: A Division of Random House, 1987.

Dinkmeyer, Dr. Don and Dr. Gary D. McKay. *Raising a Responsible Child: Practical Steps to Successful Family Relationships*. New York: Simon and Schuster Trade (Fireside), 1982.

Donin, Rabbi Hayim Halevy. *To Raise a Jewish Child: A Guide for Parents*. N.Y.: Basic Books, Inc., Publishers, 1991.

Faber, Adele and Elaine Mazlish. *How To Talk So Kids Will Listen and Listen So Kids Will Talk*. New York: Avon Books, 1980.

Ginott, Dr. Haim G. *Between Parent and Child*. New York, N.Y.: The Macmillan Company, 1965.

Gootman, Marilyn E. "How to Teach Your Children Discipline." National Committee for Prevention of Child Abuse, 332 S. Michigan Ave., Suite 1600, Chicago, IL 60604, (312) 663-3520.

"Plain Talk About Adolescence." National Institute of Mental Health, Division of Communications and Education, Plain Talk Series, Ruth Kay, Editor. U.S. Department of Health and Human Services, Alcohol, Drug Abuse, and Mental Health Administration, 5600 Fishers Lane, Rockville, MD 20857.

Snyder, Judy. *I Told You a Million Times. . . . Building Self-Esteem in Young Children Through Discipline*. Cary, Illinois: Family Connection Publications, 1989.

Strassfeld, Sharon and Kathy Green. *The Jewish Family Book*. New York: Bantam Books, 1981. "Adolescents: Letting Go," pp. 319–329.

Even "Normal" Families Need Help Now and Then

Diamant, Anita and Howard Cooper. *Living a Jewish Life: Jewish Traditions, Customs and Values for Today's Families*. New York: Harper Collins Publishers, Inc., 1991.

Doft, Norma, Ph.D., with Barbara Aria. *When Your Child Needs Help: A Parent's Guide to Therapy for Children*. New York: Harmony Books, 1992.

Donin, Rabbi Hayim Halevy. *To Be a Jew: A Guide to Jewish Observance in Contemporary Life*. New York: Basic Books, a Division of Harper Collins Publishers, Inc., 1991.

Minuchin, Salvador. *Family Healing: Strategies for Hope and Understanding*. New York: A Touchstone Book, Simon and Schuster, 1993.

The Power of Laughter

Ausubel, Nathan, ed. *A Treasury of Jewish Humor*. New York: Paperback Library, Doubleday and Company, Inc., 1951.

Gross, David C. *Laughing through the Years: A New Treasury of Jewish Humor*. New York: Walker and Company, 1992.

Learsi, Rufus. *Filled with Laughter: A Fiesta of Jewish Folk Humor*. New York: Thomas Yoseloff, 1961.

Novak, William and Moshe Waldoks. *Big Book of Jewish Humor*. New York: Harper Collins Publishers, Inc., 1981.

Spalding, Henry. *Encyclopedia of Jewish Humor from Biblical Times to the Modern Age*. New York: Jonathan David Publishers, 1969.

———. *A Treasure Trove of American Jewish Humor*. Middle Village, N.Y.: Jonathan David Publishers, Inc., 1976.

Telushkin, Joseph. *Jewish Humor: What the Best Jewish Jokes Say About the Jews*. New York: William Morrow and Company, Inc., 1992.

Money Matters

Arnow, David. "Reflections on the Family, Tzedakah, and Transmitting Jewish Values." *Sh'ma: A Journal of Jewish Responsibility*, November 12, 1993. 99 Park Ave., Suite S-300, New York, NY 10016-1599.

Estess, Patricia Schiff and Irving Barocas. *Kids, Money and Values: Creative Ways to Teach Your Kids About Money*. Cincinnati, Ohio: Betterway Books, 1994.

Godfrey, Neale S. and Caroline Edwards. *Money Doesn't Grow on Trees: A Parent's Guide to Raising Financially Responsible Children*. New York: Simon and Schuster, 1994.

Margulies, Donald. *The Loman Family Picnic*. Dramatists Play Service, Inc., 1994, 440 Park Ave. South, New York, NY 10016, (212) 683-8960.

Mellan, Olivia. "Finding Balance in Your *Moneylife*" and *Money Harmony: Resolving Money Conflicts in Your Life and Relationships*. New York: Walker and Company. Olivia Mellan and Associates, Inc., 2607 Connecticut Ave., N.W., Washington, DC 20008-1522, (202) 483-2660.

Siegel, Danny. *Gym Shoes and Irises (Personalized Tzedakah)*. Book One and Book Two. Spring Valley, New York: The Town House Press, 1982.

Strassfeld, Sharon and Kathy Green. *The Jewish Family Book*. New York: Bantam Books, 1981. "Talking with Our Children about Money," pp. 245–261.

Talking with Your Child about Sexuality

Abrams, Rabbi Judith Z. and Dr. Steven A. Abrams. *Jewish Parenting: Rabbinic Insights*. Northvale, N.J.: Jason Aronson, Inc., 1994.

Borowitz, Eugene B. *Choosing a Sex Ethic: A Jewish Inquiry*. New York: Schocken Books for B'nai Brith Hillel Foundations, 1969.

Calderone, Mary and Eric Johnson. *The Family Book about Sexuality*. New York: Harper and Row, 1981.

Gitchel, Sam and Lorri Foster. *Let's Talk about Sex: A Guide for Parents and Kids 9–12*. Santa Cruz, CA: Network Publications.

Gittelsohn, Rabbi Roland B. *Love in Your Life: A Jewish View of Teenage Sexuality*. New York: UAHC Press, 1991.

———. *Love, Sex, and Marriage: A Jewish View*. New York: Union of American Hebrew Congregations (New Edition), 1980.

Gochros, Jean. *What To Say After You Clear Your Throat*. Press Pacifica, P.O. Box 1227, Kailua, Hawaii 96734, 1980.

"How to Talk with Your Child about Sexuality: A Parent's Guide." Planned Parenthood Federation of America, Inc., 810 Seventh Avenue, New York, N.Y. 10019, (212) 541-7800.

Ratner, Marilyn and Susan Chamlin. *Straight Talk: Sexuality Education for Parents and Kids 4–7*. Santa Cruz, CA: Network Publications, 1985.

Strassfeld, Sharon and Kathy Green. *The Jewish Family Book*. New York: Bantam Books, 1981. "Talking with Our Children about Sex," pp. 239–244.

Escaping from the Body Trap

Eating Disorders Awareness and Prevention (EDAP). 603 Stewart Street, Suite 803, Seattle, WA 98101, (206) 382-3587.

"Eating Disorders: Questions and Answers," Eating Disorders Programs, Sheppard Pratt Hospital, 6501 N. Charles Street, Baltimore, MD 21285-6815, (410) 938-5000.

Fairburn, Dr. Christopher. *Overcoming Binge Eating.* New York: Guilford Publications, 1995.

Kano, Susan. *Making Peace with Food: Freeing Yourself from the Diet-Weight Obsession.* New York: Harper Collins Publishers, Inc., 1989.

Maryland Association for Anorexia Nervosa and Bulimia, Inc. (MAANA). 6501 N. Charles Street, P.O. Box 6815, Baltimore, MD 21285-6815, (410) 938-3000 ext. 3199.

Roth, Geneen. *Why Weight? A Guide to Ending Compulsive Eating.* New York: Penguin Books, 1989.

Siegel, Michele, Drisman, et al. *Surviving an Eating Disorder: Strategies for Family and Friends.* New York: Harper Collins Publishers, Inc., 1988.

Zerbe, Kathryn J., M.D. *The Body Betrayed: Women, Eating Disorders and Treatment.* Washington, D.C.: American Psychiatric Press, Inc., 1993.

Is It Love or Is It Spoiling?

Gosman, Fred G. *Spoiled Rotten: Today's Children and How to Change Them.* New York: Warner Books, 1990.

Kornhaber, Arthur, M.D. *Between Parents and Grandparents: How to Make Relationships Work.* New York: St. Martin's Press, 1986.

Trelease, Jim. *The Read-Aloud Handbook.* New York: Penguin Books, 1979, 1982.

White, Burton L. *Raising a Happy, Unspoiled Child.* New York: A Fireside Book, Simon and Schuster, 1994.

To Tell or Not To Tell?

Balter, Dr. Lawrence. *"Not in Front of the Children . . ." How to Talk to Your Child About Tough Family Matters.* New York: Viking, 1993.

Bettelheim, Bruno. *A Good Enough Parent.* N.Y.: Vintage Books, A Division of Random House, 1987.

Steinitz, Dr. Lucy Y. and David M. Szonyi, eds. *Living After the Holocaust: Reflections by Children of Survivors in America*. Revised Second Edition. N.Y.: Bloch Publishing Company, 1979.

Falling Stars and Earthly Models

B'nai Brith Great Books Series. Washington, D.C.: B'nai Brith Department of Adult Education, 1964. Volumes 1–3 (*Great Jewish Personalities of Ancient and Medieval Times, Great Jewish Personalities of Modern Times, Great Jewish Thinkers of the Twentieth Century*).

Chafets, Ze'ev. *Heroes and Hustlers, Hard Hats and Holy Men: Inside the New Israel*. New York: William Morrow and Company, Inc., 1986.

International Hebrew Heritage Library. Miami, Florida: International Book Corporation, 1969. Volumes 3–10 (*Great Jews in Art, Jewish Nobel Prize Winners, Great Jews in Science, Great Jews in Performing Arts, Great Jewish Military Heroes, Great Jewish Statesmen, Great Sages of Judaism, Great Jews in Sports*).

Kurshan, Neil. *Raising Your Child to be a Mensch*. New York: Atheneum, Macmillan Publishing Company, 1987.

Moline, Rabbi Jack. *Jewish Leadership and Heroism*. New York: United Synagogue of America Department of Youth Activities, 1987.

Reuben, Rabbi Steven Carr, Ph.D. *Raising Jewish Children in a Contemporary World*. Rocklin, CA: Prima Publishing, 1992.

Schulman, Michael and Eva Mekler. *Bringing Up a Moral Child*. New York: Doubleday, 1985.

Siegel, Danny. *Munbaz II and Other Mitzvah Heroes*. Spring Valley, New York: The Town House Press.

Slater, Elinor and Robert Slater. *Great Jewish Women*. Middle Village, New York: Jonathan David Publishers, 1994.

Weilerstein, Sadie Rose. *Jewish Heroes*. New York: United Synagogue Commission on Jewish Education, 1953 (Book One), 1964 (Book Two).

Making the High Holidays Meaningful for Children

Abrams, Judith. Family Services for Selichot, Rosh Hashanah, and Yom Kippur, with cassette, "High Holidays in Song" by Frances T. Goldman. Rockville, MD: Kar-Ben Copies, Inc.

Chanover, Dr. Hyman. *Home Start*. West Orange, N.J.: Behrman House (800) 221-2755. (A package of materials on the Jewish holidays for grades nursery—2 for use in school and at home, with parent handbook.)

Coles, Robert. *The Spiritual Life of Children*. Boston: Houghton Mifflin Company, 1990.

Kushner, Rabbi Harold S. *When Children Ask About God*. New York: Schocken Books, 1989.

Silberman, Shoshana. *Tiku Shofar: A High Holy Day Mahzor and Source Book for Students and Family*. New York: United Synagogue of Conservative Judaism's Commission on Jewish Education.

Children's Literature

Cohen, Barbara. *First Fast*. New York: Union of American Hebrew Congregations, 1987.

Cohen, Floreva. *Sneakers to Shul*. New York: Board of Jewish Education of Greater New York, 1978.

Kimmel, Eric A. *Days of Awe: Stories for Rosh Hashanah and Yom Kippur*. New York: Puffin Books, 1993.

Levin, Carol. *A Rosh Hashanah Walk*. Rockville, MD: Kar-Ben Copies, Inc., 1987.

Saypol, Judith and Madeline Wikler. *My Very Own Rosh Hashanah and My Very Own Yom Kippur*. Rockville, MD: Kar-Ben Copies, Inc., 1978.

Of Turkey and Tension

Bland, Helen Baine and Mary Seehafer Sears. *Celebrating Family Traditions: An Idea and Keepsake Book*. Boston: A Bulfinch Press Book, Little, Brown and Company, 1993.

Brinn, Ruth Esrig. *Jewish Holiday Crafts for Little Hands*. Rockville, MD: Kar-Ben Copies, Inc., 1993.

Eyre, Linda and Richard. *3 Steps to a Strong Family*. New York: Simon and Schuster, 1994.

Kaplan, Mordecai M., J. Paul Williams, and Eugene Kohn. *The Faith of America: Readings, Songs, and Prayers for the Celebration of American Holidays*. New York: The Reconstructionist Press, 1951.

Scharfstein, Sol. *Let's Do a Mitzvah!* Hoboken, N.J.: KTAV Publishing House, Inc., 1986.

Siegel, Danny. *Mitzvahs*. Spring Grove, N.Y.: Town House Press, Inc.

The December Dilemma

Donin, Rabbi Hayim Halevy. *To Raise a Jewish Child: A Guide for Parents*. New York: Basic Books, 1991.

Petsonk, Judy and Jim Remsen. *The Intermarriage Handbook: A Guide for Jews and Christians*. New York: Arbor House, 1988.

Prager, Dennis. "Raising a Jewish Child in a Christian Society" and "Raising a Jewish Child in a Secular Society," *Ultimate Issues*, 10573 Pico Blvd., #171, Los Angeles, CA 90064.

Reuben, Rabbi Steven Carr, Ph.D. *Raising Jewish Children in a Contemporary World*. Rocklin, CA: Prima Publishing, 1992.

Strassfeld, Sharon and Kathy Green. *The Jewish Family Book*. New York: Bantam Books, 1981. "Hanukah and Christmas: Living in Two Cultures," pp. 233–238.

Wolfson, Dr. Ron. *The Art of Jewish Living: Hanukkah*. A Project of The Federation of Jewish Men's Clubs and The University of Judaism. New York: The Federation of Jewish Men's Clubs, 1990.

Gifts of Love

Chenfeld, Mimi Brodsky. *Creative Activities for Young Children*. New York: Harcourt Brace Jovanovich, Inc., 1983.

Lipson, Eden Ross. *The New York Times Parent's Guide to the Best Books for Children*. New York: Times Books, a division of Random House, Inc., 1988.

Wolfson, Dr. Ron. *The Art of Jewish Living: Hanukkah.* New York: The Federation of Jewish Men's Clubs. (A project of The Federation of Jewish Men's Clubs and The University of Judaism), 1990.

Children's Literature

Adler, David A. *Jewish Holiday Fun.* Rockville, MD: Kar-Ben Copies, Inc.

Rosenberg, Amye. *Tzedakah.* West Orange, N.J.: Behrman House.

Sherman, Eileen Bluestone. *The Odd Potato.* Rockville, MD: Kar-Ben Copies, 1984.

Siegel, Danny. *Tell Me a Mitzvah: Little and Big Ways to Repair the World.* Rockville, MD: Kar-Ben Copies, 1993.

So Many Hamans. . . Helping Young Children Respond to Anti-Semitism

Anti-Defamation League—Selected Publications and Programs: "Confronting Anti-Semitism: A Family Awareness Workshop," "Confronting Anti-Semitism: Guidelines for the Jewish Community," "Confronting Anti-Semitism: Guidelines for Jewish Parents," Campus Kit: "Countering Anti-Semitism, Racism, and Extremist Propaganda," "A World of Difference Institute." ADL, 823 United Nations Plaza, New York, N.Y. 10017.

Prager, Dennis and Joseph Telushkin. *Why the Jews? The Reason for Antisemitism.* New York: Simon & Schuster, Inc., 1983.

Rosman, Rabbi Steven M., Kerry M. Olitzky, and David P. Kasakove. *When Your Jewish Child Asks Why: Answers for Tough Questions.* Hoboken, N.J.: KTAV Publishing House, Inc., 1993.

Schulweis, Harold M. "Cursing Haman, Blessing Mordecai" in *In God's Mirror: Reflections and Essays.* Hoboken, N.J: KTAV Publishing House, Inc., in association with CLAL, The National Jewish Center for Learning and Leadership, N.Y., N.Y., 1990.

For Teenagers

Bush, Lawrence. *Rooftop Secrets and Other Stories of Anti-Semitism.* New York, N.Y.: UAHC, 1986. (With Teacher's Guide by Sherry Blumberg)

Elkins, Dov Peretz, ed. *Glad to Be Me: Building Self-Esteem in Yourself and Others.* Englewood Cliffs, N.J.: Prentice-Hall, Inc., 1976.

———. *Loving My Jewishness.* Rochester, N.Y.: Growth Associates, Human Relations Publishers and Consultants, 1978.

Penslar, Derek J. *Anti-Semitism: The Jewish Response.* West Orange, N.J.: Behrman House, Inc., 1989

Werk, Susan & Rabbi Shelley Kniaz. *Figuring It Out Together: Why Be Jewish? What's the Gain, the Pride, the Joy?* A Program of Family Study and Experiences. New York, N.Y.: The United Synagogue of Conservative Judaism Commission on Jewish Education, 1995.

Passover: Opening the Door to Children's Questions

Abrams, Rabbi Judith Z. and Dr. Steven A. Abrams. *Jewish Parenting: Rabbinic Insights.* Northvale, N.J.: Jason Aronson, Inc., 1994.

Brazelton, T. Berry, M.D. *Touchpoints: Your Child's Emotional and Behavioral Development.* New York: Addison-Wesley Publishing Company, 1992.

Fitzpatrick, Jean Grasso. *Small Wonder: How to Answer Your Child's Impossible Questions About Life.* New York: Penguin Books, 1994.

Rabinowicz, Rachel Anne, ed. *Passover Haggadah: The Feast of Freedom.* New York: The Rabbinical Assembly, 1982.

Silberman, Shoshana. *A Family Haggadah.* Rockville, MD: Kar-Ben Copies, Inc., 1987.

Wolfson, Dr. Ron. *The Art of Jewish Living: The Passover Seder.* New York: The Federation of Jewish Men's Clubs. A Project of The Federation of Jewish Men's Clubs and the University of Judaism, 1985.

Making the Most of Summer

Bergstrom, Dr. Joan. *School's Out! Resources for Your Child's Time.* Berkeley, CA: Ten Speed Press, 1992.

Bloomfield, Brynna C. and Jane M. Moskowitz. *Travelling Jewish in America for Business and Pleasure.* Lodi, N.J.: Wandering You Press, 1987.

Herron, Rita B. *Surviving Summer With Kids.* Saratoga, CA: R & E Publishers, 1993.

Israelowitz, Oscar. *The Complete United States Jewish Travel Guide.* Brooklyn, New York: Israelowitz Publishing, P.O. Box 228, Brooklyn, NY 11229, (718) 951-7072, 1993.

Massil, Stephen W., ed. *Jewish Travel Guide 1995.* Published in association with *The Jewish Chronicle*, London. Essex, England: Vallentine Mitchell and Company Ltd. Distributed in the USA and Canada by Sepher Hermon Press, Inc., 1265 46th Street, Brooklyn, N.Y. 11219, (718) 972-9101.

Rich, Dorothy. *Mega Skills: How Families Can Help Children Succeed in School and Beyond.* National Education Association Edition. Boston: Houghton Mifflin Company, 1988. Chapter 19: "Special Times: Vacation/Holiday Learning."

Tigay, Alan M., ed. *The Jewish Traveler: Hadassah Magazine's Guide to the World's Jewish Communities and Sights.* Northvale, NJ: Jason Aronson, 1994.

Surviving Summer Camp

American Camping Association Guide to Accredited Camps, (issued yearly) 5000 State Road 67 North, Martinsville, IN 46151-7902, (317) 342-8456, Book store 1-800-428-CAMP.

Association of Jewish Sponsored Camps Directory (An allied beneficiary of the UJA-Federation of New York), 130 East 59th St., New York, NY 10022, (212) 836-1645. Information and Referral Service, (212) 753-2288. Directory covers camps in the Northeastern U.S.A.

Jewish Community Centers Association of North American Resident Camp List, Camping Department, 15 East 26 St., New York, N.Y. 10010-1579, (212) 532-4949. Lists camps in the U.S.A.

The Israel Experience—1996 Complete Guide, American Zionist Youth Foundation, 110 E. 59th Street, NY, NY 10022, 1-800-27-ISRAEL / (212) 339-6916 - West Coast office, (213) 655-6804.

Peterson's Summer Opportunities for Kids and Teenagers, American Camping Association, 5000 State Road 67 North, Martinsville, IN 46151-7902, (317) 342-8456, Book store 1-800-428-CAMP.

Call your local Jewish Community Center for summer camp information.

Focus on Fatherhood

Erikson, Erik. *Childhood and Society.* New York: Norton, 1963.

Furman, Erna. *Helping Young Children Grow.* Madison, CT: International Universities Press, 1987.

Goldman, Ari. "Jewish Fathering" in *The Hadassah Magazine Jewish Parenting Book,* Roselyn Bell (ed.), New York: The Free Press, A Division of Macmillan, Inc., 1989, pp. 38–41.

Gould, Jonathan W., Ph.D. and Robert E. Gunther. *Reinventing Fatherhood.* Blue Ridge Summit, PA: TAB Books (A Division of McGraw-Hill, Inc.), 1993.

Israel, Rabbi Richard J. Letters to his daughter in Riemer, Jack and Nathaniel Stampfer. *So That Your Values Live On: Ethical Wills and How to Prepare Them.* Woodstock, VT: Jewish Lights Publishing, 1991.

Marzollo, Jean. *Fathers and Babies: How Babies Grow and What They Need from you from Birth to 18 Months.* New York: Harper Collins Publishers, 1993.

Osherson, Samuel. *Finding Our Fathers.* New York: Fawcett Columbine, 1987.

Pittman, Frank, M.D. "The Masculine Mystique." *Networker,* May–June 1990, 40–52.

Sachs, Brad, Ph.D. *Things Just Haven't Been the Same: Making the Transition from Marriage to Parenthood.* New York: William Morrow, 1992.

Shapiro, Jerrold L. *The Measure of a Man: Becoming the Father You Wish Your Father Had Been.* New York: Delacorte Press, 1993.

Sullivan, S. Adams. *The Father's Almanac.* New York, NY: Doubleday and Company, Inc., 1980.

Holding On and Letting Go: How to Build a Healthy Relationship with Your Adult Child

Adams, Jane. *I'm Still Your Mother: How to Get Along with Your Grown-Up Children for the Rest of Your Life.* New York: Delacorte Press, 1994.

Blidstein, Gerald. *Honor Thy Father and Mother: Filial Responsibility in Jewish Law and Ethics.* Hoboken, N.J.: Ktav Publishing House, Inc., 1975.

Harder, Arlene. *Letting Go of Our Adult Children: When What We Do is Never Enough.* Holbrook, Massachusetts: Bob Adams, Inc., 1994.

Nerin, William F. *You Can't Grow Up 'til You Go Back Home—A Safe Journey to See Your Parents as Human.* New York: Crossroad, 1993.

Strassfeld, Sharon and Kathy Green. *The Jewish Family Book.* New York: Bantam Books, 1981. "Adolescents: Letting Go," pp.319–329.

L'Dor Va-Dor: From Generation to Generation

Foundation for Grandparenting, 5 Casa del Oro Lane, Sante Fe, NM 87505.

Jarvik, Lissy, M.D. and Gary Small, M.D. *Parentcare: A Commonsense Guide for Adult Children.* New York: Crown Publishers, Inc., 1988.

Kornhaber, Arthur, M.D. *Between Parents and Grandparents: How to Make Family Relationships Work.* New York: St. Martin's Press, 1986.

———— with Sondra Forsyth. *Grandparent Power!* New York: Crown Publishers, Inc., 1994.

———— and Kenneth L. Woodward. *Grandparents, Grandchildren—The Vital Connection.* New Brunswick, NJ: Transaction Publications, 1991.

Moldeven, Meyer. *Write Stories to Me, Grandpa! Creating and Illustrating Read-Aloud Letter Stories for Your Young Grandchild.* Del Mar, CA: Moldeven Publishing/Consulting, 1987.

Children's Literature

Eisenberg, Phyllis Rose. *A Mitzvah Is Something Special.* New York: Harper and Row, 1978.

Ganz, Yaffa. *Me and My Bubby, My Zeidy and Me.* New York: Feldheim Publishers, 1990.

Hurwitz, Hilda Abramson and Hope R. Wasburn. Ed. Mara Wasburn. *Dear Hope . . . Love, Grandma.* Los Angeles: Alef Design Group, 1993.

LeShan, Eda. *Grandparents: A Special Kind of Love.* New York: Macmillan, 1984.

Snyder, Carol. *God Must Like Cookies, Too.* Philadelphia: Jewish Publication Society, 1993.

The Book is Never Closed: Grandparents Dealing with the Repercussions of Divorce and Intermarriage

Bayme, Steven and Gladys Rosen, eds. *The Jewish Family and Jewish Continuity.* Hoboken, NJ.: KTAV Publishing House, Inc., 1994.

Cherlin, Andrew J. and Frank F. Furstenberg, Jr. *The New American Grandparent: A Place in the Family, A Life Apart.* Cambridge, Massachusetts: Harvard University Press, 1992.

Cohen, Joan Schrager. *Helping Your Grandchildren Through Their Parents' Divorce.* New York: Walker and Company, 1994.

Epstein, Lawrence J. *Conversion to Judaism: A Guidebook.* Northvale, N.J.: Jason Aronson, Inc., 1994.

LeShan, Eda. *Grandparenting in a Changing World.* New York: Newmarket Press, 1993.

Levin, Sunie. *Mingled Roots: A Guide for Jewish Grandparents of Interfaith Children.* Washington, D.C.: B'nai B'rith Women, 1991.

Myrowitz, Catherine Hall. *Finding a Home for the Soul: Interviews with Converts to Judaism.* Northvale, N.J.: Jason Aronson, Inc., 1995.

Sacks, David G. *Welcoming the Intermarried into Your Jewish Family.* New York: The Jewish Outreach Institute, 1995.

Silverstein, Alan. *Preserving Jewishness in Your Family After Intermarriage Has Occurred.* Northvale, New Jersey: Jason Aronson, Inc., 1995.

Parenting Our Parents

Blidstein, Gerald. *Honor Thy Father and Mother: Filial Responsibility in Jewish Law and Ethics.* Hoboken, N.J.: Ktav Publishing House, Inc., 1975.

Butler, Robert N., M.D. *Why Survive? Being Old in America.* New York: Harper and Row, 1975.

Horne, Jo. *Care-Giving—Helping an Aging Loved One.* American Association of Retired Persons. Glenview, Illinois: Scott Foresman and Company, 1985.

Jarvik, Lissy M.D. and Gary Small, M.D. *Parentcare: A Commonsense Guide for Adult Children.* New York: Crown Publishers, Inc., 1988.

Silverstone, Barbara and Helen Kandel Hyman. *You and Your Aging Parent: The Modern Family's Guide to Emotional, Physical, and Financial Problems.* New York: Pantheon Books, 1982.